About the Author

I had a good childhood. But then my dad went bankrupt, and my parents' marriage collapsed. Suddenly there was nothing. It was a hard time. But through them, I learned to overcome obstacles, take care of myself and accept with humility what life threw at me. I went from being a scared boy to a life optimist. I love reading; I love discovering and co-creating new technologies. I believe in: people, energy, the universe, God. That faith drives me on and is reflected in my books. I love active life, I have big visions, plans and goals, but I now understand that family is the foundation of happiness. Therefore, I am looking for a way to combine relationships and business, to be myself still and not miss the most beautiful moments with my beloved family

FIRST TIME DAD

David Vais

FIRST TIME DAD

Vanguard Press

VANGUARD PAPERBACK

© Copyright **2023**
David Vais

The right of David Vais to be identified as author of
this work has been asserted by him in accordance with the
Copyright, Designs and Patents Act 1988.

All Rights Reserved

No reproduction, copy or transmission of this publication
may be made without written permission.
No paragraph of this publication may be reproduced,
copied or transmitted save with the written permission of the
publisher, or in accordance with the provisions
of the Copyright Act 1956 (as amended).

Any person who commits any unauthorised act in relation to
this publication may be liable to criminal
prosecution and civil claims for damages.

A CIP catalogue record for this title is
available from the British Library.

ISBN 978 1 80016 685 1

*Vanguard Press is an imprint of
Pegasus Elliot Mackenzie Publishers Ltd.*
www.pegasuspublishers.com

First Published in 2023

**Vanguard Press
Sheraton House Castle Park
Cambridge England**

Printed & Bound in Great Britain

Dedication

I want to dedicate this book to my two beautiful girls and my beloved wife. You are the light of my life, my daily inspiration, and the reason I look forward to each new morning. As hard as some days are, the love I can give to you and the love I receive from you is all I could ever ask. You make me a happy man.

PREFACE

There seems to be a whole new lot of species of men, who decide to quit their jobs or take paternity leave in order to assume a role that used to be exclusively played by mothers on maternity leave. These new paternal care-givers, sometimes unwillingly become full-time fathers and take on the crucial job of being the most important person in a newborn's life. However, this doesn't reflect the situation a large majority of new fathers will experience. In most cases, a man will still spend a lot of his time at work, struggling to meet twenty-first century society's high demands placed on the head of a family. And frankly, that's not much fun at all.

Personally speaking, I was initially a complete failure. For the first couple of weeks, I was swamped with negative emotions, exhaustion and a disturbing sense of disharmony. Admittedly, I felt that way already before our daughter's birth, but after the birth those feelings really took over. I decided to do a bit of research, reading and talking with parents who had more experience than I did, which turned out to have a highly therapeutic effect on me. Once I began asking questions, though, I soon realised that no one seemed especially eager to discuss any negative aspects of parenting openly, despite its brutal life-changing characteristics.

"Something's not right," I thought. To my mind, it is vitally important to be aware of both the ups and downs of being a father. If you know what's coming, you can prepare yourself better. Just remember that most of the time things won't be too bad, which is why I decided to share my experiences with those of you who still have ambitions for their lives, and for others who are ready to settle down and raise a family. I dedicate this book to everyone who cares!

This is a message to every man who desires to become a great father and support his family, yet still craves a chance to fulfill his dreams.

A word on the fifth reprint and international edition of *First Time Dad*

Less than seven years. Exactly eighty-two months. A long time for some, a blink for others. That's how long it took to turn the world upside down. Four times in a row. The first upheaval was personal. Nina was born. Our beloved firstborn daughter, who took us out of our comfort zone and confronted us with the harsh realities of parenthood. It was a trial by fire. We had beautiful but challenging, strange, sometimes scary and, most importantly, brand new moments. Finding the balance has not been easy. But it was.

First Time Dad shows part of this path. The next piece of it, my maturation of my thoughts and settling into the role of a loving dad and good man (my ultimate life goal), can be found in another book. David Vais, dad has come a long way in these seven years. If I could send a message to my seven-years-younger self, if I could give him some advice to make his adaptation to the role of caring dad a little easier, I would have said, "Breathe. Relax. Slow down. Stop." It sounds trivial, but that's exactly what I was missing at the time of writing *First Time Dad*. Perspective.

The world around us was moving at its usual pace, but for us the flow of time had stopped. In our arms we held a beautiful, healthy baby girl, whom we were extremely excited about, but still groping for answers. Ninuška cried until the house shook. She was blubbering, raging. Later, she suffered night terrors and frequent illnesses. And my reactions to these situations matched my experience at the time. Maturity, if you will. If I had been able to stop, to concentrate, the passage through the first weeks and months would have been smoother. Still, I won't change anything about the content of *First Time Dad*. Not a comma.

As much as I would tolerate some of the situations described in the book better today, and perhaps act differently, the uniqueness of *First Time Dad* lies in its authentic description of the events around me. And because I believe that inside, at the very core, I am still the same, driven by kindness, goodness and love, all the conclusions and recommendations provided in *First Time Dad* remain valid as well. In any given situation and in any given moment. After all, most of the reviews from you, the readers, mention the book's usefulness in those difficult first weeks and months.

If you have a different view on some situations, if some of the advice and some of my views at the time don't suit you, go one paragraph further. After all, you don't have to agree with everything. You don't have to follow every recommendation. Choose what works for you. And let go of what doesn't fit. *First Time Dad* ends with Nina's first birthday. The epilogue provides insight into year two. But the world is turned on its head again with the arrival of Stella. Our second daughter doesn't throw up, sleeps beautifully, and seems calm and composed.

But even she has her days. Plus, the new situation has to be handled by two adults and one child. It's different, perhaps you could say easier, but crises still come. And then they go away. That's another book. And a little bit about turn number three. Covid. In the spring of 2020, the world woke up to a new normal. People were passing out in the streets, intensive care units were full of staff in spacesuits. The borders, the skies and some businesses closed. Fear and panic reigned.

Lockdown has become a natural part of our lives. When it worked, people breathed a sigh of relief, relaxed, a whiff of the old life came. And then boom. Wave number two. Lockdown, fatigue, exhaustion, death. Release and another lockdown. Vaccination efforts and developmental sprints yielded results. One vaccine approved, then another, and another, and another, and another. People breathed a sigh of relief. The world will be right again. In the beginning, there were lines for vaccines. But a lot of people don't buy into hard data and scientific analysis. They say they're right.

Just when it looks like the covid will enter an endemic phase and it will be possible to start tackling the huge public deficits and opening up the world, Russia decides to present its version of the truth to Ukraine. It is based on the infinite ego of a leader who takes what he wants, intimidates others with nuclear weapons and murders soldiers in the invaded country, but with them women and children. Dads, grandfathers, grandmothers, fathers, grandchildren. In the final stages of the epidemic, the world is on the threshold of a global conflict that, in the worst case, threatens to bring about the end of civilisation. And why?

Because one deranged leader and his gang could not accept that the world is constantly evolving and changing and that the only sustainable principle of existence is empathy and cooperation. We are not Americans, Germans, Czechs, Australians, Brits, South Africans... but human beings. We are one human race, with a beautiful planet dropped in our laps, which we have a duty to care for (and each other) in order to preserve life. If there is no place to live, there will be no life itself. So, in the face of the greatest aggression in decades, many people will revise their values.

Again. If you have to ask yourself quite seriously at night before you go to bed whether you will see your children in the morning, you will begin to look at your physical existence differently each day. The idea that a person stuck in the past, obsessed with turning back time at any cost, will end the lives of all subsequent and current generations, is not easy to process. The sense of absolute loss of control over the lives and deaths of our loved ones drives one into a corner. And it can cause serious psychological problems.

But we can also come away from all this stronger. And because history tends to show that everyone gets what they deserve in the end, I believe that as a society we will emerge from the events of 2020, 2021, 2022 and beyond stronger and more balanced. Family, as well as strong relationships of partnership and friendship, will be where they belong in the value ladder. In the highest positions. Understanding, appreciation, respect, humility and commitment combined with a clear vision will help us to direct our attention and energy correctly. I mean all of us, the people.

Instead of seeking out the enemy, instead of local strife and quarrels, we choose to live in harmony, freedom and prosperity on a planet that is not suffering but thriving. Does that sound too sunny to you? Why is that? Isn't that exactly the goal of every living being? To live in peace and prosperity in a healthy environment with loved ones by our side? No, this is not utopia. In fact, there's no reason why we can't achieve it. We just need to learn to lead by example much more, judge less, understand differences and promote diversity.

And the foundation of all this is found in our circle of loved ones, in our family. Harvard University's longest-running study ('The Study of Adult Development') has shown that a happy and healthy life is closely linked to the quality of relationships. Position, success, money, fame, none of these have as much impact on people's happiness, joy and health as relationships, according to the results of this study. Finally, being the richest person in the cemetery didn't make anyone happy. Let's study, let's do business, let's explore, let's innovate, let's travel, let's enrich each other.

But above all, let us love our children, our partners, our parents, our extended family, and respect each other with all our hearts. Getting into a harmonious balance in the family, but also at work and in life in general, is not easy. Balance is something one seeks, if one tries hard, one will find it, but sooner or later one will lose it and have to look for it again. Gradually, however, they will get so much better at it that each new search will be shorter and more pleasant. And on this path to balance, you may discover infinite happiness. I wish it for you from the bottom of my heart.

Your David Vais.

Chapter 1
THANK YOU

By purchasing this book, you have made sixteen months of work worthwhile. I used to stay up late at night staring at my computer screen, enjoying those rare moments of peace and quiet, far away from the everyday madness and my own personal struggle with becoming a father. Twelve months after my daughter was born those night writing sessions ended. That's when the multi-tasking editing, design, web creation and marketing process began. To put it simply, putting together a cogent e-book, or even a hardcover book with a good old smell, takes plenty of time and money.

I thank you for your understanding and appreciation.

Chapter 2
WHOM THIS BOOK IS INTENDED FOR

For those who live active, exciting lives.

Do you enjoy travelling, sports and culture? In other words, do you like to live life to the fullest? In that case, this is an ideal book for you, because all of that will end abruptly during your first months of fatherhood and you had better be prepared for it.

For guys, who want to be part of it all, one option is to simply to avoid those tough first twelve months. Stay late at work, make sure to go on long business trips, and do just about anything to avoid hearing your baby cry, having to change shit-filled diapers or having to confront any other types of 'negative' daddy duties. However, if that's your idea of fatherhood, please throw this book into the trash right away, you are merely wasting your time by reading it. On the other hand, those of you who want to cherish wonderful memories of the first months of their baby's life forever, this book will hopefully be educational and inspiring at the same time.

For women who long to understand a man's point of view.

For nine months, within a mother's womb, a new life is forming and growing. It's the woman who has to suffer from morning sickness, gain up to twenty-five kilos in weight, put up with back pain and embarrassing maternal health problems and then, on top of it all, survive giving birth. No man can ever understand what a pregnant woman has to go through and what changes occur in her body and mind before and after birth. However, high demands of the modern age don't make it too easy for us men, either. We're expected to provide for our families to the highest standards, be compassionate as well as good looking, help with household chores and be completely devoted to our families at all times.

The endless list of demands on a modern man is in constant growth. That's the reason I believe it's beneficial for young mothers to understand the male perspective, at least a little bit. Maybe they don't have the perfect partners, but those men are doing their best to maximise the synergies on their journey through family life. Despite all the effort it takes to cope with all that monotonous early parenting, these men should never give up on their great ambitions.

Chapter 3
THE ROUGH START

As an untrained driver, if you were to abruptly change direction in a high-speed Formula One racing car, you would most probably pass out due to the immense centrifugal forces. When you brake hard and sharply, it knocks the wind out of you, too. When my daughter was born, I felt such emotions run throughout my body. Even though I was in regular contact with children over the past three years through family and friends, it did little to nothing in order to prepare me for what was coming the day my two girls came home from the hospital.

What had been a comfortable life with sufficient money, an intense working pace, but also with a reasonable amount of leisure time for sports, my wife, and our shared hobbies, suddenly disappeared. Everything I knew until then ended in a fraction of a minute, suddenly and unexpectedly. It almost felt like joining a boot camp. Though I had fully prepared myself with information and advice from prenatal classes, I found myself confronted with moments that frightened me to death, unable to deal with them physically, or even worse, mentally.

I discovered that my life was slowly beginning to fill with despair, a feeling only magnified by the realisation that my wife (in my view a genetically programmed and already perfect mother) was developing a similar negative attitude. Our naively imagined dream of a contented and happy couple with an angelic, smiling baby that slept peacefully throughout the night without crying, quickly dissolved like ice on a hot summer day. And dissolving with it was our foolish illusion of a family paradise.

Unfortunately, nothing helped to prepare me for this scenario. I had the feeling that someone had put an embargo on expressing any negative sensations associated with the rough first stages of parenthood. Not in one of the thousands of Internet articles or cleverly deceptive books, does anyone openly discuss the difficult transition from being a husband to becoming a father. A relationship between me and my newborn baby had begun to form the moment she opened her eyes and was placed in my arms! To make matters even worse, something about my wife was beginning to change as well.

Hormonal imbalances in the female body following birth (postpartum blues), my own psychosis of becoming a first time dad and the inability to soothe an endlessly crying baby simply broke me. I was incapable of understanding why no previous father had enough balls to tell the world that parenting plainly sucks. So, to fill that glaring gap, I decided to tackle the problem head-on. I began to write down my feelings, day after day. I observed, examined, studied, asked questions and actually asked my wife about it. Every day I clenched my teeth, helped to take care of our newborn, and wrote down what was happening around me.

I battled on. I kept up a constant search for kindness, understanding and love inside of me, over and over again. Sometimes everything went well, sometimes less so, yet, after a series of dreadful days, something beautiful happened. Slowly, almost imperceptibly, the entire situation began to change. A feeling of inner happiness grew, as did the love for the brand-new life that had arisen from the union of two loving human beings. The result was that after several really tough months, I finally felt like I had managed to become a 'real' father. Some days a rather nervous one, but always loving, kind and willing.

The horror I experienced in those first days and weeks has grown into a quite entertaining ride with plenty of fun and humorous stops along the way. That is what will remain in your memory and your heart for the rest of your life. Parenting, more than anything else including business making, has been shown to be the only true way towards happiness. Do yourself a favour as you read on, and always remember that it will get better. Even if it seems you won't survive the day.

PERSONAL OPINION: GENERALISATIONS

I don't intend to spread fears by overly generalising. On the contrary, I would like to encourage everyone to realise that whatever happens today is only one step away from becoming better and more beautiful tomorrow. A good friend of mine and a lovely human being, warned me at the very beginning of my paternal journey, "A child that doesn't cry is a myth. Whoever claims their children are always calm and peaceful is either describing some unnatural phenomenon or is simply bullshitting you."

You will find many wannabe heroes among your buddies, who look like they got hit by a train in the first few weeks after birth, yet still claim that everything is fine and their baby is an angel. Many people may feel ashamed to admit that the whole 'new baby' chaos is simply overwhelming them. Others may be completely chilled out, perhaps because their baby is in fact a fantastic sleeper, or maybe because they just don't do much at home. For them, you can always hope that their share of hardship will catch up on them at a later stage, such as when their baby's teeth start to come in. Be that as it may, every parent will eventually face all the many challenges a baby brings into a home, ranging from gassy tummies to discovering their bodies and surroundings or to shaping their own tiny, yet individual personalities.

Although it was often a tough job, sooner or later every dad I talked to eventually admitted going through the same sorts of feelings and problems described in this book. Every one of them had to deal with the new situation alone and, in most cases, had to teach themselves to be good parents, because they were not prepared for it. And this is what I would like to change. Perhaps I'm going to generalise a little bit, although with the best possible intentions. I realise that every child is unique and exceptional, just the same as every dad and every mom have unique and exceptional personalities.

Chapter 4
PHASE ZERO: STOP THINKIG ABOUT PREGNANCY AS A FORM OF PREPARATION

This may be a slight exaggeration, although in fact all the lousy jobs requiring little or no physical effort, combined with rather bad eating habits and too much partying, have a big impact on our male fertility. Having a reliable source of information about artificial insemination, I have managed to gather a great deal of information regarding this matter. And frankly, our future prospects aren't exactly the best. Nevertheless, if you are reading this book, you are either expecting your first baby or you are considering making your partner pregnant, in which case I wish you good fortune and great success. Either way, you should be aware of the following important fact: neither the pregnancy nor the birth itself will really mean much. At least not in a way that helps you get ready to become a father. Simply because nothing very much is going to change in the next nine months of pregnancy, at least not for you personally.

You're going to do exactly what you have been doing until now, and you're even going to have sex. In other words, most times, you'll wake up to live your normal and happy daily life. It is your other half who will suffer more than you. What may slightly interrupt your own usual routine for a time is her morning sickness or heartburn. High blood pressure will take a turn during the later stage of pregnancy, as well as getting dressed which is likely to take much longer than usual, and walking more than just a short distance could also become slightly more difficult for her.

All above mentioned are some severe fuck ups we've had to deal with as parents, and I must say it was often one better than the other.

Hormone level changes = mood swings. At one moment she seems happy, which swiftly changes to being grumpy. Then she loves you with all her heart and the next thing you know, you're being hit in the head with a baseball bat.

Back pain. Because having a 'bun in the oven' is hard work. **Heartburn**. Be prepared for this. Since the baby shoves itself to every free cavity where all the internal organs are normally found, which may cause severe discomfort for the soon-to-be-mother. **High blood pressure**. This could become a serious concern for some pregnant women later in the pregnancy. **Morning sickness.**

MAKE YOURSELVES HAPPY: DONT THROW YOUR MONEY DOWN THE DRAIN

Let me tell you something about money and buying all of the much-needed infant goods. All these preparations for your long-awaited newborn are pretty tough financial times, since this can quickly run into thousands of euros, dollars or pounds, and it doesn't even really matter if your baby has already been born or is still on its way.

What is important is the fact that you're about to change your status from a childless to an expecting couple (i.e. on Facebook) and that's where it all begins. The so-called nesting syndrome somehow possesses a mother-to-be and her sudden maximum levels of endorphins will wipe out any objective perception when recognising the difference between the useless and the necessary. You will be overwhelmed by adverts offering millions of useless products that your newborn baby supposedly cannot live without, while your pregnant partner is being swamped with countless Instagram accounts of ultramodern mothers, who long to achieve inner spiritual contentment by focusing on purchasing the latest and most expensive baby fads.

Admittedly, I agreed to buy an immense amount of things that proved to have very little or no use or would stop working shortly after the purchase. For the same, or even less, money I could have quite frankly invested in something else or at least gone out to enjoy a nice meal. Below is a list of things bought during a period of twenty-two months and my opinion of them.

Pushchair / baby buggy / stroller: I have to say I have no regrets in investing money in a good buggy. It's almost like a good car. You can make a compromise and buy a better one rather than just the average car. The mere thought that you decided to go for the average car will make your ride seemingly less enjoyable and you shall soon find yourself dreaming about the better car anyway. Eventually you end up buying it, which will lead to spending twice as much money than you would have, had you gone with your first choice right at the beginning. Surely, it won't be any different in the case of a buggy. Some particular brands maintain their price value, and therefore there is little to no money to be lost during its one to two years in use. Of course, the cost is at first higher, but they provide much greater comfort to both you and your baby and when they are no longer of any use, they can be sold for only about ten to fifteen per cent less than the retail price. As for low-cost buggies, you usually find yourself losing up to sisty per cent of the retail price.

Heart rate monitors and standard baby monitors: quite honestly, having read many reviews on all kinds of baby monitors, I decided to invest in one of the more expensive options: Angel Care video types. They proved to be a very bad investment. The alarm would go off too often and the product doesn't work very well over a longer distance. Generally speaking, the product doesn't live up to its expense. As for the breathing monitor, you may be either relaxed or perhaps even more stressed by it. Eventually it will end up back in its original box, just like our one did. You will most likely begin to monitor the baby yourself and this will completely change your mindset. Find the full review on my website.

Cute infant clothing: the worst mistake of all. Talking about the first twelve months, we had an unlimited supply of clothing. Imagine all the much-needed cute baby clothes, even though much of it will not have any use at all, because your baby will grow inevitably and incredibly fast. Especially if your little one persistently vomits, then it's impossible to keep up with the constant clothing changes. To my mind, clothes worth having are pure cotton baby bodies, a large supply of cloth nappies and a small number of pretty items to wear like a sweater, a little hat or a cute jacket. When in the buggy, your baby will be all wrapped up and not much of the clothes can be seen anyway, while at home it will spend most of time in the overalls. Although if you insist on purchasing all the cheeky clothing items available on the market, perhaps you should consider beginning your purchases for your baby's first birthday.

Baby swing chair: once I felt at the end of my wits, which made me buy the perfect remote controlled baby swing, some sort of a baby shaker. I was imagining this as an easy way towards better sleep for the whole family and finally getting some time to recover. However, I can't exactly say that Nina particularly enjoyed this and she used it only several times. It can work sometimes, but I wouldn't give it much thought. Therefore, if you consider purchasing one, do yourself a favour and focus on the least expensive ones. It's highly unlikely to ever make the cost of it back when reselling it later.

Toys: I have noticed something pretty distressing. In many cases it's actually parents buying toys for themselves, rather than for their children. Most often their own nostalgia leads them to falsely believe their children's life depends on this particular purchase. All you have to do is to be careful and you will naturally reduce the amount of toys in accordance to your baby's needs and interests. Generally speaking, it's the simplest toys that make children happy and you are less likely to become a complete lunatic.

Chapter 5
THIS IS WHERE IT ALL BEGINS

The way I had imagined it was to stand by my wife, and just hold her hands and her head. If there is something I remember from all the childbirth classes, it is 'silence is golden', especially when it comes to giving birth. But that wasn't our case, since the only people in the delivery room were the midwife, my wife and me, therefore my hands were of much higher importance than I had ever expected. Instead of standing by her side, I suddenly found myself pretty much delivering the baby. I had been warned about the trauma of seeing my wife give birth and how I would never get that sight out of my mind and my entire opinion of women and female genitals will change forever. But that didn't happen either.

Following the birth, my wife was totally exhausted. We had an extremely quick delivery that only took around four hours, followed up by a not exactly compassionate roommate and her loudly bawling baby.

Second day's visit was about six hours long with baby Nina sleeping throughout most of it. Upon my return home I received a text message from my wife saying Nina was sweet and quiet, which was exactly what I hoped for.

Third day felt like hell. Nina was screaming, wouldn't sleep and my wife didn't have any breast milk. I fell into a depression.

Fourth day seemed better, although not much. I kept assuring myself everything will be all right, and we will make some sort of a system in order to cope with things.

Fifth day, they are finally back home. Here come the first changes. Just remember that it all begins with giving birth. It may remind you of the last three months of pregnancy, which was already tiring, exhausting and annoying, simply because your wife was no longer able to move around well, all of it was accompanied by mood swings and morning sickness. But as soon as your wife gives birth, all those inconveniences go away. This is where the new chapter of your life begins, and after the first one comes another. Your very reason for being alive is about to change, as well as your way of thinking and you will find a whole new meaning to your life. It all begins with the birth.

Chapter 6
FIRST MONTH: I WANT TO TAKE IT BACK

At the beginning, Nina was sleeping quite well, in approximately three to four hourly long intervals. Then she had some food and it would usually take her some time to fall back to sleep. The first night we stayed up bursting with adrenalin. We had no idea what was coming, with absolutely no one around to help or give us some advice. All we needed were hospital nurses to make it possible for us to have a three-hour nap while the baby screamed into their faces.

After three days, Nina's sleep cycles shortened. Especially the length of her night sleep is much shorter. She screams, makes horrific noises and constantly squirms around. I recall what one mother wrote on an online forum: *Newborns are like little animals*. And they are exactly that. They rattle, grizzle and pant loudly. It may be normal, and at times it seems rather understandable. Having only just been born, babies have to adapt to the new environment. It's coming at them all at once and it requires a lot of time to get accustomed to.

Over the coming days, our sleep deprivation gets worse, and so does our sense of hopelessness. I was praying for a restful baby but there was a tiny Satan on Red Bull growing inside of my daughter instead.

It's official. Our old life is gone and both my wife and I fell into depression. Although we love our little baby girl, we are now forced to stay at home. We hear a baby crying everywhere we go and we would love to soothe her, but we don't know how. We are hopeless.

Nina's bed seems like a prison. She has difficulty falling asleep and even though my wife has enough breast milk, we are considering getting more supplies. Perhaps some sleep might save us. Every night I have all kinds of thoughts on my mind. I found myself looking for a solution to a problem which seemingly couldn't be solved. Only several weeks later did I realise that I was trying to solve a problem that didn't even exist.

I'm not able to work from home even though I can. During the day I can't get anything done at all, there is no regeneration during the night and so with every new day my ability to execute all my working duties rapidly decreases. "m worried about my daughter and my wife and I feel upset because of how exhausted she is. All my work projects are on standby while the finances are just floating by.

My wife and I talk every day. We share our feelings, we read stories about other people's experiences and we seek the positive side of our situation, but at the moment none of this helps.

I must have read about a thousand articles since our baby girl was born. Every time Nina coughs a tiny baby cough, it drives me back to pages of online forums or Facebook groups. The current situation turned me into purchasing a typical American bestseller about a perfect baby that never cries. This is the baby I longed for, where is it then? Suggestions from the book are not working. The American dream in your bed? I don't think so. Once at night I got awakened when the breathing monitor went off and I remember thinking I was dying.

So far, we have only been out twice for a walk. Romantic walks with the buggy while holding hands, all smiles and spasms of happiness are nowhere to be found. Instead I get stomach cramps every time we try to get out. I'm frightened that every time we go out it ends up with loud crying and running back towards home.

I'm talking to other, more experienced, fathers and I even call my sister, a great mother, several times a week. Before that, we would speak less than once a month. I feel so grateful for every little bit of help or advice. In fact, the only thing I'm really seeking is an assurance that we are not alone in this and that we are going through a standard transition into parenthood and that can be painful.

The sleepless nights and exhaustion made me damage both my cars outside my house. At first I call myself an idiot, but only moments later I'm seeking some kind of a message in my wrongdoing. "Stop thinking nonsense and be grateful for your healthy daughter and a family," I tell myself.

I tried so hard to live by this motto, until the following night. Nina's hysterical crying and her screams were so strong that I could feel vibrations in my brain. I was picking up the pacifier to calm her, but at the same time there was a lot of anger building up inside me. I tried all kinds of swinging positions in my arms and even tossed her around at one point. At the end of two hours of battling, Nina had a massive poop and finally fell asleep next to her mother and we swapped two hours later. The way I look at it now is that every new day brings some kind of a victory.

There is nothing in the world I wish more than to enjoy this time. It only comes once in your life and it can never be recovered or taken away, but no matter how hard I try, I can't do it at the moment.

Finally, the time has come and something has changed. I recall going somewhere by car, and Nina was sound asleep throughout the entire trip. I took her for a walk in the buggy and she was still sleeping very deeply.

SUMMARY OF THE FIRST MONTH. **WE SURVIVED.**

My depressions come and go. Sometimes I feel jaded, completely exhausted and shocked, with mixed emotions. Nina looks like an angel when she is asleep. Several times before she had slept for up to four hours. She sleeps mainly in the baby car seat, as well as in her buggy and luckily for us, sometimes in bed. This is usually followed up with another crisis with hardly any sleep, lots of crying and hysterics without any possible reason. These are the annoying moments for me. Doesn't she have everything she needs?

All in all, we are slowly starting to adapt to the change. Nina has gained one kilo in weight within three weeks, which I'm rather pleased about. It was only a few days ago when my wife and I were considering phasing out breastfeeding. Absolutely determined it was about time we started feeding Nina with powder milk, I stormed the supermarket with a vision of a perfectly restful night. I'm not at all sure my plan would have worked, although my wife didn't agree with the idea anyway, so we continued with breastfeeding.

MY SUGGESTIONS FOR THE FIRST MONTH

Think positive: I know this is easier said than done, but you have to try. Remember, it will get better, maybe not now or tomorrow, but it will. Just remind yourself that this not so enjoyable period will soon be gone and the wonderful days, months and years are soon to come.

Don't let it slip through your fingers: time goes fast. The sense of helplessness caused by your sleep deprivation might make you seek a way out of reality. I suggest you take a nap in the office and quickly run back home as soon as possible. Your baby will reach one year of age at a breakneck speed and you can never retrieve all that time back again. The bad memories will blow away, while the good stay with you forever.

Divide responsibilities and tasks: plan in a sense that, 'you do this and I do that and we will swap tomorrow'. Both you and your partner need some time off.

If you can, go to work and avoid working from home: should you not be able to do so, be prepared to exert tremendous effort, because the advantage of working in the office is that you return home fresh with no concerns about the baby. You will be able to change the nappies, swing or play with your children, while your wife gets some well-deserved rest.

PERSONAL OPINION: THE BABY AND BUSINESS.

For the first time since Nina's birth, I went on a business trip. How incredibly refreshing, inspiring and even profitable this was, especially when it comes to the family. It's lovely to get back to your normal life that doesn't only involve changing nappies or putting your children to sleep. It just means you can finally enjoy some rest. Furthermore, this business trip also assured me that men shouldn't take paternity leave. At least the vast majority of men.

If you are dreaming of changing the world, achieving great things and have big ambitions in order to lead a fulfilling and happy life, staying at home isn't exactly your plan, paternity leave may not be the best thing to do. Luckily enough, my wife's love for Nina has grown about a hundred per cent deeper and she has an incredible ability to deal with things with empathy and complete tranquility.

All this allowed me to get back to work and there is so much joy in what I do. New opportunities arise, my visions and ambitions are back and I have regained my commitment towards the family and my intentions are to have a good financial backup, big enough for new experiences and travelling.

Chapter 7
SECOND MONTH: UP AND DOWN, AND SOMETIMES TO THE RIGHT

I must say that we have a rather sensitive baby. On the other hand it's no wonder, since both her parents are very spiritual and sensitive human beings. Our lives are filled with intangible assets, and our baby girl has inherited some of our own attributes and characteristics. It will certainly come in handy to her, but at the same time it may not always be so easy on her journey through life. You can see her obvious sensitivity simply from the way she reacts to sounds. Nina is still deeply dependent on her mother, but she is finally becoming more at ease in her father's presence, or rather Dad is still learning to relax with his little daughter. Nonetheless, it's a considerable change compared to the early days, and parenthood is starting to take over my heart.

There still hasn't been much of an improvement when it comes to sleeping, however. I have sensibly decided to spend the nights in a different room and my wife is dealing with all the night issues alone. I feel slightly upset about this situation, but there is no chance of getting any sleep in the same room with that little creature. The moment she starts to move around or make some of her weird little noises I mentioned earlier, my night is over. We have been trying very hard to find a way of swapping around Nina's day and night sleeping patterns, but unfortunately without a success. During the day she has no problems falling asleep at least for a couple of hours, be it in the car or in the buggy. Everything changes once the clock hits midnight, and it starts all over, just when her parents start to feel really worn out.

One would almost say things were beginning to improve. Nina was sleeping for up to five hours at a stretch and my wife seemed to have caught her second wind. She was so optimistic and happy, full of zeal and contentment and suddenly it's all gone as soon as Nina's sleep rhythm drops back to only one and a half to two and a half hours. We try to get her to sleep from around ten p.m., which usually takes between one to three hours. All the while she grunts and twists, makes horrible sounds that leave me separated from my wife for the night. I have a very bad transition from light to deep sleep, and Noisy Nina's gasping and whinging quickly has me on tenterhooks.

Still, we are slowly getting closer to the romantic strolls with a buggy we have always dreamed of. Not only do our walks last longer, but we start to enjoy them and are no longer terrified of Nina's hysterics. The buggy has become our daughter's favourite place to be and she has learned to snooze while being pushed around. Unfortunately, taking part in any sport activity in general has completely vanished from my life since there is absolutely no time for it. My life has somewhat turned into one continuous turbulence. Lots of ups and downs which, in regards to the baby, means that one time her hysterical crying and bad mood cause me a splitting headache and the next time I don't mind her moaning at all.

One way or another, our baby girl has made such a great improvement, which is what keeps me going. The biggest step is indeed her increasing ability to observe her surroundings. She no longer gives a kind of uninterested and bored look, but she is now looking around with curiosity. Besides all the happiness, sorrow, fears or pain, it's the purity and beauty that I see in her eyes. Her eyes begin to make connections with mine and they tell what her lips can't say just yet. There is so much in Nina's eyes that I enjoy looking at. Even though she still hasn't developed the ability to smile, I recall her first laugh. It happened while she was asleep and it suddenly made us forget about her mood swings.

Finally, after having been isolated for weeks, we received our first visit, which Nina didn't particularly enjoy and she cried the whole time. After being asked whether, "It's always like this", I once again fell into a slight state of depression from the so-called early days.

I felt once again frightened about an evil baby whose parents end up on antidepressants.

And since the next couple of nights went particularly badly, all the negative thoughts drove my wife into saying, "Why didn't anyone mention this? Why didn't anyone tell me how extremely exhausting this would be? That I won't be able to get much sleep and will be dreadfully tired all the time? I'm fading away, I can't do it any more. Had I known this, I would have waited a little longer."

I must admit I felt exactly the same way. On one hand, it's wonderful having a healthy baby, but what's harder is that we had no idea about all the aspects of the early stages, and that this will be turning back and forward and the improvement is nowhere near in sight.

And then it happened. Nina started to smile, so beautifully and disarmingly, with complete innocence. Even though she still can't keep a smile on her face for very long and she has an incredible ability to switch to hysterical yelling within seconds, you can't get the smile out of your head. More importantly, this tiny human creature senses perfectly when it's the right time to show her smile. Just about when you are feeling down and tired, and you once again find yourself thinking about asking someone to babysit, she stops crying, smiles at you and your heart begins to melt. The entire survival of the human race comes down to this powerful weapon of a child's smile and in a modern society it's quite likely helping to keep up some natural population growth. Were it not for children's smiles, the entire demographics of the Western population would have declined long time ago.

PERSONAL OPINION: ALL ABOUT THE DEMOGRAPHIC TREND

It's a great paradox that the evolution of society and the entire Industrial Revolution together with building a better tomorrow and making immense amounts of money, generated all sorts of weird possessions we would not imagine to live without. We desperately need shopping malls, restaurants, cinemas, theatres, exhibitions, gigs, experiences, massages, cosmetic salons, gyms and bars and all that. Our entire lives depend on all types of things which people in the past wouldn't even imagine. And, unless we get what we consider the essential part of our being, we slowly start to fall apart.

I'm a perfect example of this. I have spent the past ten years of my life completely occupied. Admittedly, I really enjoy what I do and it hasn't always been only for the money. Most importantly, it was the joy, ambition and my determination to succeed. And then suddenly everything changed and my goals turned to possessions, which usually comprised of four wheels, and mostly I really ended up buying them.

Eventually I bought my own apartment and then more and more wheels, many experiences and a huge supply of technology products. Sadly, my unconditional love for all things material deprived me of what our ancestors had a long time ago, which was the ability to adapt to such a change as a new family status. Back then, a mother would start wearing the baby in a sling shortly after giving birth to handle all her daily tasks. There was a close contact between the child and its mother and the baby would be easily accepted into the world of grown-ups.

When the mother wasn't around, it was either the grandmother, aunts or other children who took over the baby care. Today our worlds collapse when we find out how our new life completely starts to drift away from the old one, originally full of comfort and amusements. But habit is second nature and it's difficult to instantly shift around your own mindset onto the next, more sensible chapter of your life. We have somehow forgotten the fact that having a baby also means losing some of the freedom and comfort we used to have, but that is a natural part of it all.

By now, we have consistently transferred to intermittent vomiting, the nappies absorb tons of pee every day, but the poop is nowhere to be found. All our troubles in the last couple of days were related to pooping, which rapidly started to get worse over the next few days. As soon as milk reached Nina's stomach, it was quickly followed up by monstrous farting and we could start changing the nappies. Only during the past two weeks has Nina's pooping eliminated into longer intervals, until she would only poop once a day. Soon after it stopped, and there was nothing.

There was a tiny stain in the nappy on Thursday with almost nothing on Friday, and absolutely nothing from Saturday until Sunday midnight. On Sunday afternoon I started to panic as Nina was trying to arduously push it out. She tried so hard that at one point it seemed her eyes were about to pop out, but it was all to no avail. Due to this unhappy new experience, she went slightly hysterical on Friday and it became worse on Saturday. On Sunday she stopped fighting it and her battle was resumed later in the afternoon.

Her worried father decided to once again skim through the pages of social media, learn about other mothers' (fathers, where have you gone?) dismays and literally took last resorts in the sugarless organic laxative, chamomile tea, to come into use. But most importantly, I made my way to the pharmacy. After hearing all about our issues, the lady behind the counter immediately gave me remedies for gas relief. I reacted with, "Thanks but really this isn't what we need. My daughter farts like an old man. She tries very hard to push it out, but she still can't do it."

The lady shrugged her shoulders and suggested we go see a doctor. Seriously? I decided to use the community's know-how and asked for a rectal tube. In the evening we gave Nina a warm bath with some chamomile tea followed up with use of the tube. At first there was nothing, but Nina eventually let out some sort of a 'mash'. I could fully understand that this tiny creature had no clue how to deal with this thick dry glue. There wasn't much of it that came out, but still it made me think how fortunate this moment was, when suddenly it happened. Something that sounded like a fart, smelled like rotten eggs and, all of a sudden, we had an enormous poop and a very happy Nina.

Is there anything that can be done to prevent situations like this one? According to the doctors, after the first six weeks, breast milk's consistency changes and the infant's digestive system develops, which leads to decreased bowel movement. On one hand, our doctor suggests we avoid the rectal tube, but on the other, according to experienced mothers, during a baby's first three months a rectal tube is a savior. Although I'm not eagerly convinced which is the best solution, we have decided to let nature take its course, unless there is an interval of one week's length.

SUMMARY OF THE SECOND MONTH. **STILL GOING.**

Assuming that you are still adapting and getting used to the change, both good and bad days come regularly, but it still isn't comfortable enough. Today our baby sleeps, tomorrow she doesn't, while her dad seems to want to sleep nearly all the time. Other men are either spending the night in a different room, like me, or they are lucky enough to have a deep sleep.

When it comes to Nina's upbringing, we try to set down some rules. We bathe her every day and we try to do it earlier in the evening than before. We also do a lot of regular muscle exercises and massages, in order to help Nina's digestion. This follows up with breastfeeding, cuddling and then sleeping.

Sometimes she sleeps for up to five hours with a record of five and half hours being the longest. However, after a restful night usually comes one when my wife doesn't get much sleep and has to get up nearly every hour. Basically, it's all one big chaos.

We've also had our first refusal to drink milk, which only lasted one afternoon, but quite understandably made my wife cry. Nina was rather hysterically screaming her heart out the whole time. She wouldn't eat or sleep and surprisingly she didn't even want to play. All of these factors belong to the second month of adapting to this brand-new way of living.

SUGGESTIONS FOR THE SECOND MONTH

Focus on the positive perspective: of course, the first three weeks of a child's life in this world are so intense they may seem like years. In order to maintain good mental health, I suggest you focus mainly on the positive moments. Just enjoy it with all your heart and keep it in your back pocket to remind yourself when your little one starts to get on your nerves. All the nice memories will help you overcome the weariness and anger, no matter the cause.

Chapter 8
THIRD MONTH: WHERE THE HELL HAS ALL MY TRANQUILITY GONE?

At the beginning, the system we have laid down worked for well for everyone… apart from Nina. In the daytime she sleeps in short intervals, which typically take thirty minutes up to an hour. Our little girl requires a lot of entertainment and she constantly observes her surroundings. Melodies and a teddy bear both became her favourites. She is probably thinking something like, "All right, Daddy and Mummy, I will be nice and cute and I might even smile at you with a big grin on my face, but don't expect me to do it all the time. I'll wait for about twenty minutes and then I want to be grumpy again… this is so boring!" More screaming and yelling. "Come on you two, entertain me or you'll have me yelling and crying all over again!" The way my wife tries to deal with such situations is by singing and talking to Nina, which is what I try to do as well. I have even tried to take her for a little tour around the house in my arms, although our six rooms, including the bathroom and an office room, doesn't seem to keep her engaged long enough. As for the playing blanket, that seems to only work for a limited amount of time. What seems to be helpful is the television, although we aim to leave it off the schedule, since Nina has her entire life in front of her to watch television.

Sleep deprivation is perhaps the worst of all. At night our daughter wakes up every two hours, which doesn't give my wife enough time to reach any form of deep relaxation. Despite the fact she is dreadfully tired and exhausted, she can't get to sleep in the afternoon either, since Daddy goes to work and there is nobody else to look after the baby. My big responsibility is to make sure I can fund our family life and keep the business going, so I'm fairly often on the go and my wife is dealing with the tasks at home. I recently told my wife, "Darling, one day I shall build you a memorial as a form of respect to every woman on maternity leave out there. Because honestly, it's like having two full time jobs at once."

SPECIAL OPINION: RITUALS, PART I.

I'd like to share some of my secret ways to a relaxed night. According to my own research, there are numerous factors involved and it may take some strenuous effort. Fulfilling the baby's needs is vitally important:

* Your baby should be allowed some balanced breastfeeding, which means countless meals throughout the day. As soon as it starts to throw up several times in a row, it's losing some sort of balance.

* Try to prevent gas and bloating. There is nothing worse than breaking the balance. Helping your child get rid of as much gas as possible will ease your own nights.

* Your baby would have preferably pooped during the day, otherwise prepare yourself to get very little sleep during the night.

* Make sure the baby is kept warm and comfortable, as being too hot or too cold brings along another great issue.

* Both parents need to give their baby all the love there is, for if one party is not giving enough, the other has to provide for both. This is purely my point of view, although your child normally needs plenty of cuddles anyway.

* Needless to say, plan the feeding time ahead of bedtime as much as possible, in order to avoid falling asleep on an empty stomach.

Some other experienced mothers gave us another handy piece of advice to never change nappies at night. Every time we had done so, Nina got completely woken up and we never managed to put her back to sleep. Both my wife and the baby were drained without sleep, the baby was losing its balanced sleeping rhythm, with my wife not having enough space for recharging the energy she needed for the next day. Ever since we stopped changing nappies and swapped for special, highly absorbent ones, nights like these had been long gone.

Next thing we started to change was the time schedule. Our little owl creature slowly starts to learn to get up at early hours. We aim for her to take the bath between eight and nine p.m., but sometimes we used to do this at nine thirty p.m. I can clearly hear the so-called ethical mothers say, "Oh! How shocking!" But they can quite frankly kiss my butt.

Technically, at the time of my wife's pregnancy we had a rather shifted daily schedule and would sometimes go to bed at two a.m. and that is why I called our Nina 'little owl'. Below is written our step-by-step process ahead of bedtime:

Bath time helps Nina understand that bedtime is fast approaching. Put some baby cream on. We use thyme balm for her chest, belly and lower body. Head and back moves/exercises for her physiotherapy for breast feeding. We turn all the lights and TV volume down. Nina relaxes on my wife's chest until she nearly falls asleep. Nina gets carried upstairs. All is ready for sleeping.

We try to keep the daytime sleeping pattern in a similar spirit as the night-time sleep, which unfortunately doesn't always work when Nina's in the buggy. Most babies enjoy the buggy since they can be outside and they sort of wobble up and down. Perhaps the wobbling is where all the joy comes from. For example, when in the car, the baby constantly falls asleep from the up and down movement.

However, this all depends on getting enough food into the belly without having any problems with flatulence afterwards, for this could quite possibly ruin your plans. I must admit, this is something we come across rather often; we turn around and what we see is Nina sucking her dummy with her eyes wide open.

PERSONAL OPINION: WHAT THE EXPERIENCED SAY.

Experienced fathers have the following advice: try to avoid overstressing. Naturally, your second baby will grow up more independent, since it doesn't have all your control and attention as your first baby. In the book called *Originals*, the writer Adam Grant, in his countless studies and examples, points out how all children that came after your first one eventually achieve a much higher level of resourcefulness, originality and success. First children generally aim for more conservative jobs, whereas the children who come after them are the ones who push the boundaries.

It's rather simple, for when both children are crying, one of them always has to wait and it usually happens to be the oldest. Even though the younger one naturally receives more attention, it's nowhere near as much as it was given to the older one in the first place. Furthermore, as you become a more experienced parent, every little tear, whinge or fall is dealt with in more calmness from your side. While your first child is being brought up by the grown-ups, your other children grow up next to their siblings and grow more independent. All these aspects play a considerable role in developing their own character and independency and, according to Adam Grant, also individuality.

When talking about the ways of raising up and building up the relationship between you and your children, I recommend you to watch a short interview with Ashton Kutcher on *The Ellen Show*. Ashton Kutcher, who is well known for his roles in countless of romantic comedy movies, is more importantly a very successful investor in technology. Just to name a few of his investments, there are, for example, AirBnB, Optimisely and a language learning platform, Duolingo.

Not only is he an intelligent human being, but also someone with many interesting innovative thoughts. In the interview, Ashton Kutcher compares a newborn baby to a new mobile phone. It looks beautiful and brand new, but not all the functions are in working order yet. The camera doesn't work, you can't make any phone calls or send text messages. With babies it is very much the same.

As I mentioned at the beginning of my book, even though a newborn's sight nor its hearing hasn't fully developed, it somehow has to breathe, wee and poop, yet it doesn't know how to use its legs or hands and is hungry all the time. When they asked Ashton why didn't he and his partner Mila Kunis hire a nurse, he answered they want to know their child. They want to be there when the biggest changes occur and they want to share the love, as well as the pain and the only way to achieve this is to be present.

When Ellen asked Ashton was what was the most surprising thing about becoming a father, he paused and answered that it's how deep a love towards another person can be. A feeling that constantly grows past the boundaries, past anything you ever felt towards another person. He added a quote by Carlos Slim, which states that most people think they need to make a better world for their children, while the truth is that we need to make better children for our world.

The rest of the interview is slightly irrelevant to us and Ashton talks about spending most of the time at home because of the inability to go out with a buggy due to his own prominence.

Ryan Reynolds, a movie star known mainly for his comic book movies, can be often found talking about parenthood on his Twitter feed. Read his ten lessons about parenthood:

It's vastly important to teach your children how to use their imagination. His daughter often hears from him that the reason the sun goes down is because it's angry with her.

It's important to read to your kids every night.

Sooner or later when bringing up your children, you'll find yourself having no idea about what you're actually doing.

When you've not had enough sleep and the constant crying takes you to your wit's end, you're close to doing something like this.

Never judge your own parenting skills by evaluating the improvements in children around you. (Needless to say, these are very often mere theories or even made up.)

Children are like mushrooms, they absorb information very quickly.

Have enough patience and keep calm. Your life hasn't stopped because of your kids. Moreover, sometimes you may find yourself in a situation where you decide to put yourself first in order to be able to take care of your kids even better at a later time.

No matter how hopeless you feel you are at any time, always remember you would do anything for your children. There will be times you do the right thing, and then you don't. You always do your best for your children.

SUMMARY OF THIRD MONTH: **END OF THE FOURTH TRIMESTER**.

All the panting, growling and grunting from the early days are gone. Nina has a calm, happy sleep. Indeed, sometimes she breathes loudly, although it has changed and it's very innocent. These are some profound physiological changes. The expression in her eyes has dramatically changed into more focused and curious. In comparison to the early stages, her eyes no longer struggle to adapt to contrasts of light, but they start to distinguish and discover the world around her. She loves to look in the mirror, attentively stares at the TV screen and enjoys watching Mummy run around the kitchen.

She especially enjoys her toys with sounds. I must say I've had enough of the song 'Somewhere over the Rainbow' for the next ten years. And for the first time ever, our little girl laughed out loud. All we did was make silly facial expressions and dance around and both of us were bursting with laughter. The mere memory gives me goosebumps when writing about it days later. Nina's laughter does wonders after having spent the last three months in full deployment mode over her. Having children is truly wonderful, even just for the happy moments you get to spend with them.

MY SUGGESTIONS FOR THE FIRST THREE MONTHS:

Pursue your life as it was before your baby was born. Go out for a nice meal, do nice things. Not allowing your new life to entirely take over the old one will keep you on top of things and you can re-discover your old passions. Ask the grandparents to look after your little one and have some time just for yourselves or even alone, it will do you wonders. Consider it a form of recovery. Besides, that's really what this is, such a change in your life is a sort of regeneration. Perhaps you're not able to look at it from this point of view just yet, but it will change everything entirely once you accept this idea. It's all up to you, you can become the best version of yourself.

Communicate with each other. The secret lies in talking about every aspect of your new life, about the good and bad. Share it with each other and don't keep it inside you, if there is something you disagree with or you'd like your other half to change their behavior when it comes to raising the child, talk about it. Believe me, this isn't a psychological cliché, speaking out will become your savior. Dishonesty can have dreadful consequences and may eventually result in losing each other.

Chapter 9
FOURTH MONTH: NO MIRACLES

Once I came across the following statement, which I quite happily believed was true, and it's that the fourth month brings a complete breakthrough. Apparently during this month, the tiny creature, who until now was only slightly able to distinguish images, sounds and would only sleep when it's not meant to, really turns into a human being like us. The little human has, by now, fully developed its senses, smiling, the ability to sleep through the night, become a loving creature and is able to keep itself entertained when the grown-ups are occupied. A baby's development has an evolutional character and only people who don't see your baby every day actually recognise the biggest improvements. Whereas for us parents, there's a rather smooth transition between months three and four.

At least as far as we're talking about night-time, for the biggest changes come in the day. You should be able to stretch the length of sleep with all kinds of rituals. Saying that, Nina usually takes a nap three times a day for about thirty to sixty minutes. When not sleeping, she loves to discover the life around her, smiles more regularly with every new day and loves to play with her crib toys. What is being considered a significant improvement is her discovery of her own hands. This fact made her realise she can insert her entire fist in her mouth, which is very interesting to watch indeed. However, what I believe is the key development, is her relationship with us.

She is becoming more and more conscious of what is happening around her and she smiles frequently, therefore we are no longer experiencing just her meltdowns and hysteria, and the bond between us grows stronger. When the time comes and she becomes distressed again, her smile is the key factor which makes me realise my love for her grows stronger, even though sometimes she doesn't give anything back all day long. From my point of view, apart from waiting for some big breakthrough, this is a month of the bond between me and her.

It wasn't until very recently that Nina got to spend more time with Daddy, which may be down to her increasing weight and curiosity. My wife carries her around from dawn until dusk and that is when we change the guard. It has become Nina's somewhat traditional position with her head slightly pulled up in order to digest her food properly and it gets her engaged for some time. After this she starts to moan and cry, and it doesn't even help relocating her from the sofa to her playing blanket with crib toys, which doesn't keep her entertained for very long. If none of this works, we keep switching positions.

These are either the easing position, when Nina is rolled up in our arms or in exercising position, where her legs are bent and she rolls forward, or we simply cuddle her or carry her around. Apart from that, she is interested in absolutely everything, especially observing her own facial expressions in the mirror. What she finds engaging, even if just for a moment, is observing her parents, but at least she doesn't moan or cry. And indeed, it's quite hard work.

My arms, shoulders and back are sore, since in the past couple years I'd changed from going to the gym to cycling. Gone are the depressions, but they seem to have somehow turned into extreme tiredness. The way it goes is that, basically when the baby is crying and you have no clue why, your head starts to hurt and you naturally lose all your interest. All you want to do is slam the doors behind it and come back when it's all over. And you know what? There is nothing you can do, you just have to get over it. Perhaps you can do some sports, try to read or watch a film.

And since we are slowly getting closer to some raising up, my aim is to explain to my wife she should let Nina grow more independent. The baby should grow finding its own way of keeping itself engaged and prevent boredom. From now on, neither Mummy nor Daddy will come along to entertain her every time a sigh or moan is heard. This strategy has proved to be working, and she engages all parts of her body to play with and keeps herself entertained either by a toy or herself.

PERSONAL OPINION: WHAT HAPPENS WHEN DADDY'S NOT AROUND?

Neither me nor my wife have been feeling at our best lately, and my wife didn't talk about it. I noticed something wasn't right with her mood and several times I overheard how she was telling Nina to, "Be a good girl or Mummy will throw you out of the window". Which she obviously immediately denied. After returning home from my business trips, I was greeted only by an obligation. What didn't make this situation any better was tiredness caused by lack of sleep at night, everything got worse and we started to argue about what was happening. All the bad spirit was caused by my failure as a caring father. In the past two weeks, perhaps even longer, I hadn't taken care of Nina for at least an hour to give my wife some time to do anything else. I hadn't changed the nappies for about as long and didn't look after Nina from my own initiative. The truth is, I have too much on my plate and,, at the moment at work there are some radical turnovers, which require some new rules and problem solving. Unfortunately, when you're a father, you're expected to be fully engaged all the time in order to fulfil tasks, as in your normal life. After a while, my wife quite naturally begins to start going mad. Being at home with a baby is rather a monotonous activity, and since you're constantly singing, lisping and carrying a little one around, you are quite likely to have your brain melted. Therefore, I have decided to make some changes in the schedule lately and I make sure I spend more time with Nina in the evenings, change her nappies and give my wife some time for regeneration. This has proved to be greatly beneficial for my wife's well-being.

PERSONAL OPINION: RITUALS, PART II

Already four months after the birth did we start to feel mentally exhausted from the monotony of our new life. The system we have set out may help to bring some regime order to Nina's life and helps during the night, although on the other hand it has a detrimental effect on me and my wife. Especially the constant repeating of the following tasks:

Daytime breastfeeding, with exact intervals and lengths

Tummy times come ahead of certain procedures Walks outside with Nina asleep in the buggy Afternoon playtime

Evening bath time Evening breastfeeding and bedtime

A day in the life of an infant comprises of many rituals, so be prepared to start with yourselves in order to maintain consistency in the newly introduced life. One of the first things we had to change were our late evening shopping expeditions. At first, our day was spent entirely at work and grocery shopping always came late, which had a great advantage of taking as much time as we needed in this otherwise overcrowded supermarket store.

Whereas now, there is absolutely no chance. No more going to movies, spontaneous trips outside the house or weekend holidays. No more chilling and watching movies, no more time to spend alone with my wife, let alone any physical intimacy. Instead of all this, our life has entered into some kind of a monotonous stereotype. Ever since Nina was born, the so-called stereotype has a new title: "regime". Perhaps the biggest challenge is to make this stereotype somewhat creative and original and beneficial for everyone. There is nothing to worry about, the time will come.

PERSONAL OPINION: FINANCES, PRIORITIES AND WEALTH

As a child, I recall myself being pretty obsessed with Christmas and all the gifts. I never unwrapped presents slowly, it was more like tearing the wrapping paper off. My life was divided into time prior to and after Christmas, with nothing in between. When, at thirteen years of age, I was forced to start setting priorities which meant that every time I got some pocket money I immediately invested into some of my personal needs and desires such as cars or electronics, and, as the time went by, I even began investing in presents for my loved ones.

When I turned twenty-six, something happened and all my Christmas bills rapidly increased. I must admit it was very satisfying and beautiful seeing my family so grateful for all presents I bought, and my investments knew no bounds. Unfortunately, as you sow, so shall you reap and all my presents were taken for granted. This situation doesn't exactly come in handy at a time when you and your wife have just had a baby. Still, despite the investment in our home and all the equipment needed to get ready to start raising a baby, I still enjoy giving presents to others.

On the other hand, for the first time this year I have come to the conclusion that not all that glitters is gold. Having a happy baby next to me, I have suddenly come to realise that there nothing equals a family happiness. But this doesn't mean that your new life should completely stop you from remembering that the rest of your family wants and needs you. Once you've started, you can't simply ignore the financial aspect of your life and leave it behind.

Unless you're planning to travel around, buy an island and live a happy life with your own rules, entirely independent from all the outside world, then money is what you will need to get by in life. Money will bring you experiences and buy you things that will make your life so much easier or even more enjoyable. However, having spent our Christmas alone at home this year truly made me think about money as a type of tool.

My new plans are to succeed in the upcoming projects and create a solid financial basis, which means I didn't completely forget about the money-making side of my life. My aim is to make sure Nina learns to live in a modern mainstream society along with her potential siblings, but I have also realised something that I never realised before Nina was born. It's that my family always comes first, and I must say, it's a wonderful feeling.

SUMMARY OF MONTH FOUR.

Having spent our first Christmas together and on my way towards becoming a better parent, I made the following vital decisions. We have started to be very strict when it comes to some daily rituals. After taking a bath we turn the TV and lights down and move straight to breastfeeding. After feeding we hug and cuddle with Nina and take her straight to bed. Usually, breastfeeding is followed up by some incomprehensible hysterical crying, but it has sort of become a part of this whole ritual, too.

My wife no longer stays upstairs with Nina until she falls asleep as she did during the first three months, and she comes back downstairs. Nina's trouble falling asleep sometimes forces me to step in with my spartan regime, detailed step by step in crying-pacifier-cuddles and then leave her alone until I return for another round of crying-pacifier-cuddles, go away and she finally falls asleep. And it works! Those are some of the nicest moments that Nina and I have alone. This is what gives us more energy and slowly takes us back to what we miss from our old life. We still don't expect to sleep all through the night, but my wife no longer looks like she hasn't slept for days and she is finally able to perform some daily tasks.

Don't expect any miracles, at least when it comes to Christmas should it happen during the first four months of your newborn's life. But I must say our daughter seems like a rather bright child. She loves lights and colourful displays of all kinds, as well as melodies. Obviously, there was no sign of interest or excitement yet to be seen in her eyes that could be somehow related to Christmas. Even though she was only born four months ago, we still keep our hopes about her being able to share the happiness and excitement which comes along with Christmas. As much as we would love for her to be able to feel the way we do about Christmas, it's not quite possible yet. However, perhaps next year will be different.

SUGGESTIONS FOR MONTH FOUR

Be patient and think positive, work on your endurance and keep track with the daily rituals. You are the role models to your children and the bond between you and them is getting stronger. Essentially, you will find a way to your baby one way or another. No one has come to this world as an already experienced father. You just have to live through it. Take the time to create this bond.

Plan your time wisely and be available to be present when needed.

Your presence is vitally important in the evenings and late afternoons. Take walks together, help with bathing, feeding and putting the baby to sleep. Just do everything you can to let the bond between you and your children grow stronger and to give your wife some time for herself.

Try to never let go of your dreams, whether they are personal or work-related. I personally discovered that I could suddenly understand some business-related things that I had previously only thought I understood. I'm able to make use of my fatherhood experience and learn new things at work.

I have opened the doors to some of the best people in the industry to join my team and I chose people I like to work with. All I thought before – that when I have a baby, all my work will be pushed aside and I will mainly spend my time sitting on the balcony and help out with household chores from time to time – has vanished, and that's the way it should be.

Chapter 10
FIFTH MONTH: THE TIRING SYSTEM

Infants go through constant development stages within their first year on earth. Essentially, the most crucial aspects of one's development in such early life stages stay pretty much the same. My wife still gets up three to four times a night to feed Nina, who sometimes refuses to go back to sleep and stays up until four or five a.m. mumbling to herself in bed while her parents are dozing. By this time, Nina's facial expression is probably the most notable of changes to be noticed. Besides that, we have experienced the first case of flu in her life to be coped with.

Even the toughest of guys may sometimes end up in bed with a simple flu, but think of the tiny human beings, who still haven't fully mastered the common inhalation and exhalation through their nose or their mouth. The most common cures for blocked noses in babies are salt water solutions or sucking out mucus manually with a nasal mucous. You'll spend your time hoping for the cold to quickly go away while you're cleaning up vomit from the floor. But there's nothing to worry, this cold won't stick around for long.

A good thing to know is, in fact, that a cold that is not treated at all will last just as long as one that you've tried to treat with everything you can think of. In regards of Nina's new facial expression, when I recall Christmas, there was very little perception and kindness in her eyes, whereas now I feel like her eyes are able to comprehend more and more with every coming day. This evolution in her eyes allows you to recognise what she's going through and how she perceives the world around her.

She keeps turning and looking around and she tends to look down when she's not in the mood to look right at you. It is wonderful to observe this change of a tiny creature into someone you are able to communicate with. There is a channel on YouTube called *Super Simple Songs*, all sung by two talented Americans with some lovely animations for children. It's all very cute and educational, they do simple maths, learn about different types of animals and parts of the human body. I wonder what a language therapist or a pediatrician would think about them, but what matters to me is Nina's pure joy while she watches them.

She looks at it from her own point of view and perhaps it may help develop in her some interest when it comes to learning languages. Over the years I have mastered my language speaking skills and I truly enjoy speaking English. Today there are countless of great options when studying English. Nina simply loves to watch this; it keeps her entertained for thirty minutes without me doing any harm to her or forcing her into watching it. I try to keep a balanced wide range of activities and to my mind, playing with toys as well as reading books are just as important.

Another interesting facet that changed during the fifth month of Nina's life is her ability to relax. She simply enjoys being alive, which affects us as much as her, which now has a completely positive effect on us. She smiles, mumbles and kicks everything around her and starts to discover ways to crawl and generally just seems very comfortable and relaxed.

As for the crawling, we are still at an early stage and watching her crawl backwards is rather enjoyable. But, of course, hysterical crying still occurs from time to time, although more often we experience some sobbing, perhaps caused by her teeth starting to grow in. Apparently, this was precisely what our neighbor's son was going through when his teeth started to come in.

My wife and I have long discussions over this matter and seek what causes it. Perhaps we blame the time, or more particularly a start of another stage of development in Nina's first year, or perhaps it's down to nutrition. Ever since we started feeding our daughter with her first baby milk porridge about a week ago, she wouldn't stop eating. I must admit I'm not exactly delighted by the thought of my daughter eating some processed packaged food, it seems to have become her favourite meal and she appears content when going to bed.

We have decided to make some change changes in the ritual and here is how we do it. We feed the baby with some baby porridge, give her a little break after, do a bit of swinging and then we finish with breastfeeding, which is followed up by bedtime. For several days Nina hasn't had any problems falling asleep quickly, which gave me and my wife some time to be alone together. It's lovely to be lying in bed knowing your baby is happily asleep and you won't have to get up within the next five or six hours like you did during the first months of pretty hard work.

My wife no longer feels exhausted or dreadfully tired, but she seems to start being sick of being at home all the time. In order to ease her struggle and give her some time to relax and keep myself in good condition as well as keeping my mind clear, I decide to start taking Nina for long distance walks in the buggy.

PERSONAL OPINION: AN EXAMPLE OF HOW THE NEWLY INTRODUCED REGIME MAY NEGATIVELY AFFECT THE LIFE OF AN ADULT

Intend to keep yourself motivated and don't look back. While you have to be fully engaged at work, prepare yourself to be a part of some daily tasks as well as helping to keep the child's regime up and running. You won't have to undergo all of this any longer after you realise how dreadfully tired you are. You almost feel like taking time to breathe and get off the endless stereotyped cycle, but no matter how much you want it, it's not available at this stage.

While your wife looks terribly tired and beaten up with the same kind of monotony, both grandmothers have just retired and have little or no interest in helping out with a baby and you are completely worn out with no energy at all. Unluckily those are the times you start to think that 'one child is enough'. All you have to do is to stick together and raise this little creature towards your own comfort, so that you can have some time for yourself later. Next thing is to set some rules and incorporate freedom, spontaneity and infinite challenges for yourselves and with as much frequency as possible. For in such situations you will not find a magic fairy knocking on your windowsills offering help with raising your children.

Mostly it will be only you and your wife and there is not another choice other than to fight on and find the most suitable system. This will eventually lead towards a brighter future, proper sleep and less exhaustion overall. Until one day something fills you up with a relentless feeling of love and happiness. Just an old photo, a conversation, a song or a moment of being alone on a business trip. Flooded with endorphins in a strangely emotional state of mind, you forget about all your little struggles.

Suddenly your entire body tells you that absolutely nothing, no life assets, wellness packages or success can possibly compensate for this tiny human creature with the same blood as you running through its veins.

Surely, there are many people like me. As much as I love to create and invent new things, so do you. You love to push the boundaries and enjoy keeping track with new technology and inventions, feeling especially attracted to people who are part of all this.

For the past twenty years of my life, I have had a burning desire to leave behind some legacy. Elon Musk is building a rocket for international space flight because he feels responsible for the entire human race and his aim is to send people to Mars (simply because another great scientist, Stephen Hawking, only gave us another thousand years here on earth). For now, I'm not able to help Musk in achieving his goal and as much as I admire people like Musk, Bezos, Buffet, Steve Jobs or Larry Page and Sergey Brin, my life goals are quite different.

Even though the idea of conquering the world and settling on other planets than the Earth seems to be very popular among researchers and writers, there is a major problem and that is all the harm we have done to the Earth. This beautiful blue planet is in terrible danger. What upsets me is the fact that anyone here can do pretty much whatever they please, no matter how bad the impact, and without wasting a thought about what is going to happen with their inventions after people made enough money from it, and then just throw it all away.

It gets tossed into the sea, forests or fields and stays there for centuries to come. I feel responsible for this and this will become my next goal. I intend to leave this world assured that I did what I could to make the world a better and safer place.

SUMMARY OF THE FIFTH MONTH.

Just about one week before the turn of the fifth and sixth month, which we call the magical half-year, we are being more demanding and are getting used to the system which we have introduced some weeks earlier. After having tried different ways of trying to sabotage this, Nina has finally started to conform to our rules. Days strictly follow the time schedule and we scarcely go off the following path.

We get up at six a.m., although this is still more up to Nina's biological clock. Breastfeeding and a short sleep is on schedule until approximately nine a.m. It may occasionally happen that due to lack of sleep at night, Nina' s nap takes a bit longer.

Nappies get changed, my wife gets Nina dressed before putting her down on the playing blanket. Then she gets turned around and plays with her toys while laying on her back.

After playing on the blanket, Nina gets all of my wife's attention and this is followed up by a short nap time. In the meantime, she gets ready for her nap by rolling herself into the blanket alone or with a little help from her mother.

It usually goes like this two times around. Alarm clock, getting dressed, breastfeeding, play time, cuddling and then finally sleep. Providing I manage to get home on time, we all go out for a walk around three thirty p.m. Sometimes, as I mentioned earlier, I go alone with Nina to give my wife some time to recover. From this moment starts Nina's longest sleeping interval until around seven p.m. From seven p.m. onwards we try to keep her entertained as she won't go to bed right after an evening bedtime story. She gets her porridge around two hours later and takes a bath shortly after.

She finishes her evening meal with breastfeeding, which sometimes makes her fall asleep on her mother's chest. Either way the baby is then moved to her bed. Whether she is already asleep by the time we carry her upstairs or not, she will be left alone to fall asleep. There is a great advantage in laying down a system. You simply know when to expect certain changes, what works and what doesn't and what she is used to. You may be limited to some sort of a kind stereotype, while not being completely pulled away from your favourite activities.

SUGGESTIONS FOR THE FIFTH MONTH

Make some time for yourself. Your daily life should not be planned too spontaneously since all the activities are very much scheduled to a specific time. There are specific times the baby needs to sleep, how it behaves after waking up and what you can get done between the sleeping intervals.

Take time to go out and do some sports, see your friends, go to the cinema, an exhibition, concert or anything that makes you happy. Either alone or ideally together as partners, in case the grandmothers can help with the baby while you do something else.

Make an intention to lay down a system starting with the fifth month while introducing a more strict upbringing from around the first half a year. If you're lucky and your baby is smart and active enough, you will get through without losing your patience.

Remember that any exerted effort in laying down some strict time schedule and system before this time will not be very effective. While at first being utterly convinced it's possible, I was terribly wrong. Remember that our children are not going to blackmail you until they've reached a certain stage of development, so until then it's all up to the biological needs of your baby.

Chapter 11
SIXTH MONTH: NEW REALITY

I'm not even sure whether the last five months have gone quickly or not. All the negative emotions caused by horrible nightmares from the first weeks have been pushed aside, and when I recall Nina crying from ten p.m. until two a.m., it no longer feels like it was as bad as it may have seemed at the time. Perhaps it is just human nature attempting to defend itself against another reproduction. If we were to vividly remember all the negative memories, it would be unlikely humans would ever consider having another child. Not only do I agree with the idea of having another baby, but I'm also aware of the burning desire of being able to experience all the struggle again.

We have recently noticed some new emotional and physiological developments in Nina's life. The way she picks up her toys is much more coordinated than before and she is quite easily able to stuff her mouth with them. For the first time she has discovered her legs and how much fun she can have with them during all her playful activities and even during bath time. She also started to look through the baskets around the flat, throws her nappies and toys around, which gets her very confused and wondering where all the stuff has gone.

Her cries and howls are so loud it makes the windows rattle. She constantly chatters and mumbles, especially when taking a bath or while playing. To my mind, this development stage is in the form of a step-by-step guide. The purpose of this book is not to describe the entire evolution of a baby's life, as there is countless information in every clinic or on the Internet. My intentions are to make sure you enjoy this time as much as possible.

With the sixth month, also commenced the proper raising of our little girl. It makes much more sense now that she can understand what things mean and distinguish changes in the tone of my voice. Out of constant observation of Nina, we realise that what helps her distinguish new sounds and tones is by looking at us and our facial expression. For example, when hearing a new sound at home, she firstly gets frightened of something she has never heard before, until she looks at her parents. If the sound is followed by a smile on the parent's face, she gives a smile back.

Increasing the sound of our voices and a grumpy look instantly triggers lots of crying, which essentially means she will be more careful next time, or at least that is how I see it. After going through some interesting literature, we are reducing the supply of toys and the main focus is on the ones most beneficial to Nina's intellectual development.

SPECIAL OPINION: FIRST SERIOUS FLU

Nina's first serious flu interrupted our general well-being. It has been the sixth time she caught flu, although until now it has always been variations on common childhood illnesses. The way her body and mind reacted to this flu was horrific. Her glassy eyes, rubbery body and the complete resignation left her parents sleepless while constantly trying to shake off the high fever and waiting for a change for the better. Her temperature disappeared after three days and immediately turned into a rash all over Nina's body.

When the flu finally started to disappear and everything went back to normal, we realised what a negative effect this health episode had on the entire household regimen we had laid down. During her flu period, Nina was being pampered by her parents. Unless you are entertaining and carrying her wherever you go, she starts screaming and gets very agitated. To make matters worse, for whatever reason she now smiles less often than before the flu and is very moody, sometimes even annoying.

Even worse is the fact that she lost her sleep routine and again wakes up every thirty minutes throughout the night. All she had learnt and acquired before the flu was forgotten and she became a grumpy child. The situation is nowhere near to being ideal. It's very easy to forget the ever-changing aspects of having a baby at home, especially when you began to think you got through the hardest part, but this is life as we know it. We can never seem to be able to happily enjoy what we have, without any struggle and the unforeseeable events life brings just when we least expect it.

I have made some necessary arrangements and brought back our once already well-established Spartan system. Needless to say, it's only for the baby's best. And quite frankly, I decided to ignore her restlessly nervous yelling and crying unless she has a serious reason to do so and is not merely demonstrating her opposition to certain activities.

SUGGESTIONS FOR THE SIXTH MONTH

Although our system may be too harsh at times and tough for everyone involved, it has proven to work very well within our little family. Both your and your baby's life will work in keeping up with the arrangements you set up. It helps the children to understand your own expectations and system and it brings a feeling of reliable certainty into their life.

Stop thinking about the future and enjoy the moment. This is the time not to be missed. It's the time your baby smiles a lot, starts to know you and creates the bond between both parents. You can absolutely see it in their eyes, and just remember that all that happens from now on will greatly affect whatever comes next.

Organize your work-life balance according to everybody's needs and in order to prevent later regrets. Indeed, I'm part of the 'Y' generation who refuses to die in their lousy office jobs. I work a lot and I enjoy it, I know what I want from it and why I do it, which is also how I know that now is the time not to be missed.

An hour or two a day to take over from your wife's responsibilities should be exactly what she needs to recharge her batteries in order to be able to continue spreading the love towards the baby and maintain harmony at home. Simply give your wife some time.

Find someone to babysit so you can take some time off from the constant lisping, carrying, nose wiping, and vomit or poop cleaning, for otherwise you will soon lose your mind. Not only will you need moments of solitude with your own self, but also just for you and your wife. All you need is two to three hours to relax.

Chapter 12
SEVENTH MONTH: SHE'S A DARLING

The flu finally went away, our darling Nina is back and with her came some considerable physiological, as well as cognitive, developments. She started to smile again, she observes and discovers her surroundings but mainly, she is learning about herself. It's all very entertaining, rewarding and fun to watch.

Our baby, Nina, brings so much happiness into our life, so different from the one I used to miss so much in the early weeks. All of this is now a part of us, it's not just going to disappear elsewhere. This is our life now. The bond between us and Nina grows deeper and stronger. Every loving father around the world develops an instinct to protect his children and it becomes an integral part of their love.

It's such a wonderful feeling and a wonderful change that happens on your way through life, and this is exactly how Nina's seventh month went by. A rather important event from this period should be mentioned, and that is the vaccination. Apart from that, all she has learned the previous month somewhat continuously developed into this month. We were still strict when it came to rituals and time schedule, as well as enjoying our moments alone without Nina. She understands that she can pretty easily fall asleep alone without her parents being close by and she can sometimes sleep until the morning.

PERSONAL OPINION: VACCINATIONS IN ORDER TO PROTECT THE IMMUNE SYSTEM

Nina has received her first vaccination. We've decided to postpone this until she was seven months old, instead of letting the doctor give her the jab when she was only three months. The decision was made due to my research after which I have come to the following conclusion.

I firmly believe in building a strong immune system naturally and I'm well aware of how the pharmaceutical industry increases its profits. And indeed, the pressure of the stock exchange and shareholders have caused many other alarming commodities to be sold. I pay attention to all of this and I never go to a pharmacy unless it's quite necessary, as I mostly start to boost my own immune system as soon as I feel the flu coming on.

It's a perfect way to overcome any illness. Of course, my attitudes towards vaccination are not exactly positive, but on the other hand some things have to be done whether we like it or not. They are mandatory in order to protect everybody around us, as well as ourselves.

Moreover, compulsory vaccination truly helped to wipe out or eliminate some deadly diseases and the only reason why some parents can actually allow themselves to refuse to vaccinate their children is because everyone is already vaccinated. If everyone was to refuse a vaccination and attempted to fight it with natural remedies only, all the deadly diseases such as whooping cough or tetanus would make their comebacks and once again be as widespread as they were back in the day.

Of course, not everybody will be affected, but do you really want to put your children at risk and see if they are among the few not affected by the disease?

As for our family, we will almost certainly stay with the basic compulsory vaccination regime and will do our best to strengthen Nina's natural immune system so that she is able to fight every cold and flu. As for the compulsory vaccination, I completely agree that everybody should take a certain responsibility into their hands, which is why we took this prevention with Nina in a two plus one vaccination schedule.

Overall, little Nina dealt with her first vaccine with no issues and we strongly believe that next time we come face to face with flu, it will be dealt with without too much complications.

Chapter 13
EIGHTH MONTH: DADDY'S STRICT DISCIPLINE

On one hand, we got used to the way things are and, on the other hand, we learned to let things happen naturally. Nina still isn't the type of a child which sleeps from the moment you put them in bed until six a.m. Most of the time she sleeps from around ten p.m. until three a.m., which is when she starts to toss and turn or mumbles in bed for fifteen minutes until she falls asleep again. We have learned to live with this fact and we have also agreed Daddy will not interfere when it comes to Nina's midnight crying.

When experiencing some of her hysterical crying simply because she isn't getting her way, we just let her yell until she stops. By now she is clever enough to know the right time to put herself into hysterical mode and when she is merely wasting her energy. You just have to let this happen sometimes for her to realise this is the way it will be. After having spent the past seven months together every day, you should be able to recognize when something isn't right or when she is just trying to get her own way.

Either way, your child is your choice and it's up to you whether you wish to let your children take over your life from the beginning, or whether you teach them to respect certain rules. It's up to everybody to find what is most convenient for them. I have seen so many children not being able to entertain themselves unless the parents are close by for few minutes and what happens is that some parents react to every unhappy whimper with immensely exaggerated attention. As well as that, I have seen so many children who have been sleeping alone ever since they were born and they are all very independent individuals.

Simply, set down your own rules to suit your family's needs. From my point of view, there is no such universal advice that could fit everybody individually, although a wide range of all different suggestions can be found online. Your children are born with a certain personality, character and every soul suits a different need. Therefore, if you personally feel like your child may need more personal contact with you, let them stay in your bed. In case you don't, teach your children to sleep in their own room. As for our Nina, she needs a lot of personal contact and love just like any other child, although the point is to recognize the situations when it's needed most. I'm sure you will find your own system.

To my mind, it is important to teach your children to become independent by letting them play alone, let them find out that things won't always be the way they want. The combination of intuition, feelings and common sense accompanied by some Spartan bravery is perhaps the best combination of all, at least for me. But you may see things differently.

So, it happened from one day to the next that Nina started to speak. Ble, ble, bla, po, be, dada, mum, mam, and so on. Before it was a mumble here and there, whereas now she sometimes talks for ten minutes. No matter where she is, whether it's at home, in the car or when we are visiting friends or family, she smiles. She starts to be able to express her opinion. Such moments are a lot of fun to watch and somehow it is very energising.

Nina's teeth are starting to come in very rapidly. The first pointy tooth is slowly getting through her gum line, which quite naturally seems to upset Nina. If only we could go back to our infant years just for a moment to remember how unpleasant this was. Perhaps it would be helpful in order to handle our baby's annoyance, especially when an otherwise lovely baby with almost no problems sleeping, suddenly turns into a little monster baby who wakes up every thirty minutes with hysterical shouting.

But because you and your children have been living next to each other for quite some time and there are many things you have learned and found out about them, it's a good time to show your understanding and compassion and let your children know you are here for them.

PERSONAL OPINION: YOU WORK, I WORK, WE WORK

I have finally found my way back to my job, for the first time since Nina was born. However, my desire to spend most of my time with her and my family sometimes forces me to be highly over-productive. There is a lot of organizing and time management involved in my working system. I have learned to be strict when it comes to new projects with a lack of visible potential growth or projects that arise from the old ones, which require a considerable amount of effort with very little benefits and a small potential of financial growth.

To put it simply, I have learned to say NO and I use this word more and more frequently. Back in past times, I considered this a form of disrespect towards people who ask me for help or offer certain opportunities that would now make my life more difficult. After observing the wiser and more successful ones, I examine the potential growth of all projects before taking them on. No longer do I leap at every opportunity and challenge that comes my way.

First, I allow it some time, I take a closer look at the figures and observe the clients. In case I decide to commence a new project, I prefer to do it slowly, step-by-step. After establishing dimensions and creating metrics, I watch over the net amount of investment to have a certain idea about the ROI (Return Of Investment), use the MPV methods (Minimum Viable Product) as well as GH (Growth Hack Code).

I simply started to enjoy what I do and, in comparison with the past, I'm now able to leave the business behind and return home to my little girl, which I do from my own initiative and with more excitement. No longer is my life about possessions, but about the great moments we can share together. This is the main reason for my work, to support my family financially.

Chapter 14
NINTH MONTH: WE ARE SPRINTING

When it comes to our parenting development, we are making rapid improvements. I stopped counting the minutes left until the next month a long time ago. The times when I was frightened by the mere thought of the fast-approaching night are far gone, just like my fears of shopping. All just because Nina is no longer the sleeping baby, but she is interested in watching the world around her and I'm no longer frightened by her sudden waking up and yelling and crying.

My working time schedule is now between eight and ten hours a day and has been divided into several shifts. Whenever possible, I take Nina for walks in the buggy between the shifts or go cycling. I dearly missed sporting activities in my new life, and now that I can enjoy it again, it has rapidly increased in value. By now, Nina can turn herself over from her belly to her back and vice versa, and when lying on her stomach she almost looks like a miniature breakdance champion.

Until she learns how to walk, my role of the sling-carrier father remains. This has shown to be a good way to keep fit, providing your baby has reached ten kilos and you constantly move it from one arm to the other and back. It's almost like going to the gym. My biceps and shoulders haven't looked like this since I left high school.

There have been some bad days when she is working on her assault skills and sleeps less, changing into better nights when sleeping like an angel. Although every time it seems like things have become stable, frankly, it always changes. While some events in life repeatedly seem like a stereotype, the first year in the life of an infant is more like a roller coaster.

If I were to compare the journey to her first teeth, it would be steep climbing to the top and then back down, straight and then a sharp turn to the left, then right and quickly back down again. When coming to terms with teeth for the first time, it turns even the most relaxed baby immediately into a tiny beast. It certainly has to do with some character development, although these newly appeared pointy teeth explain the last several bad nights.

Moreover, Nina is growing into a very active baby, who I call my 'turbo mouse'. She moves around all the time while waving her hands and legs around, she claps, mumbles, kicks about and crawls on her hands and knees, and slowly but surely is beginning to stand up. It is when she starts to walk, that all the fun commences.

Little by little we grow more strict in her upbringing. The afternoon nap time looks like this: "Sweetheart, you're tired, let's go to bed." We give her a quick cuddle in our arms, kiss her goodnight and quickly take her to bed.

At first, she usually starts to cry, but if she is smart enough, she soon realises that Mummy and Daddy aren't coming to soothe her and falls asleep as a sign of protest. All you have to do is hang on and hold tight, until your baby learns to fall asleep even in the daytime.

I did some research about sleeping with some acquaintances and friends who are all mothers and fathers. What I have found out is that eight-to-ten-month-old children with no teeth coming in would sleep without waking up through the night. On the other hand, children with two or more teeth have similar symptoms to our Nina, which are often interrupted sleeping, constant awakening and outbursts of hysterical crying.

Our baby's teeth come in faster than the trees in spring, which causes our restless nights. However, the sooner your baby's teeth start to come in, the sooner it will be over.

PERSONAL OPINION: END OF VOMITING, END OF CLEANING

In case you were presented with a persistently vomiting baby, here is some good news for you. The vomiting and puking will eventually stop due to the development of the lower esophageal sphincter muscle. When this muscle gets to an advanced stage of development, it holds the food down in the stomach.

Whereas with babies it allows the food to travel back, and that is what causes them to puke or vomit.

From now on, unless you want to wait until they digest the food after every meal, all you need to do is give your little one a shake here and there and play around with them. But most importantly, you can forget about wiping the vomit off the floor or changing stinky nappies all the time.

Quite honestly, the end of the vomiting period has opened a new, more relaxed stage of being a father. Not only does this allow us to play around together, which is something we both enjoy very much, but it also brings one of my most unpleasant duties to an end. Even though I accepted it and learnt to live with it, I really didn't like the smell of it at all.

Chapter 15
TENTH MONTH: A SOLDIER IN THE FIELD. HE IS SHOT

Nina is discovering her knees. She gets up on her hands and knees and for now still only crawls around. She is just like a shot soldier in the field when dragging his left leg behind him. It's rather a fun thing to watch her move from one end of the room to another while only using one hand and a leg.

When on her way, she discovers all the facilities in her environment while wiping the floor with her stomach. Luckily enough, her regular vomiting stopped two weeks ago, so she isn't spreading it all over the place while moving around. And truly, this is what happens on a regular basis in other households.

Teeth are still rather a hot topic this month. They keep coming in one after another, which has a negative impact on Nina's nights and is the reason for general grumpy moods. Frankly, I'm not able to comprehend how my wife can handle all this. However, your children's teeth growth triggers some memories of situations from the early days of parenting.

The baby is having problems with sleeping, quite often cries and even shouts and is unable to stay engaged in any activity for too long. Sometimes Nina doesn't eat very well, which leads to her being hungry later, which then makes her grumpy in general.

Teeth are beasts and they take around three years to grow, with the worst period around six months long. Luckily the teething issue comes and goes, the teeth don't come in through the gums all the time, which means your baby's bad mood will come and go, and the same for you. Mummy can get some sleep, everything at home gets back to normal and you can happily enjoy your moments together once again.

PERSONAL NARRATIVE: A LOOK INTO THE FUTURE. JOHNNY AND HIS THREE-YEAR-OLD SON.

When you become a father, sometimes you quite consciously begin to ask the more experienced fathers about their own children. Generally, when you're single or only in a relationship without marriage, you don't often think about children, unless the situation becomes appropriate. Whereas, when you're a parent yourself, it becomes a subject of discussion before sports, sex or career.

Earlier today I asked my friend about his three-year-old boy and his seven-year-old daughter. The girl is doing fine and there is nothing interesting to talk about. The boy, on the other hand, according to my friend Johnny, has discovered his self-esteem together with his first period of defiance. This period includes disobedience, refusal to conform to otherwise established rules and systems, hysteria and loud, often horrible, public tantrums (when the boy starts to roll around the floor in a shop, insisting on getting his way). Another curiosity Johnny mentioned was, in fact, that his boy hasn't pooped for several weeks.

Even though his bathroom visits seemed as regular as an old guy's with prostate trouble, he couldn't push anything out, not even one little poop. This situation must have been previously discussed by some scientific study, which states that too much constipation or faeces in your bowel isn't going to help towards a good mood. Let alone when it happens to a little boy. Basically, with every new poop not coming out, the boy's mood dropped further down and the lack of sleep increased. It's nowhere near ideal to sleep constipated, with a bloated stomach and, if you're a child, you simply cry.

There are the following conclusions. On no account should this tiny body stay constipated. Don't get too excited about your standard eight hours of sleep and rest. Your child needs all your unconditional love and support throughout their entire life. Johnny, his wife and especially their little boy really stood up against it and realised that if it won't go naturally, it will have to go with a little help and the boy really pushed a few times and all their trouble suddenly went away.

Chapter 16
ELEVENTH MONTH: THE PERFECT HOLIDAY

Once I had a dream, that providing we make it through the first weeks and months of the hellish parenting, our family will go on holiday (including a crazy, sassy mother-in-law). Our little girl will soon reach her eleventh month of being on this planet and everything will be just perfect. It will be our Garden of Eden. Nina will be playing on the beach while I write one whole sunny chapter of this book, with many recommendations and suggestions about how much everything has changed compared to the horrific beginning, and the happiness will get me moving from side to side.

So, it happened and we went to Croatia. It's rather near, and the Croatian coast and its warm climate are nice. The beginning was slightly stressful due to crossing the borders to the Adriatic Sea at night, specifically heading for the island of Krk. Unlike my previous trips, I was well prepared. I took a sleeping pill in the evening ahead of the journey, napped about four hours and, around three a.m., I drank a Red Bull.

Something worked, although I'm not entirely sure what. Either it was my mindset or the Red Bull. Between four thirty a.m. and six a.m. my eyes looked like the saber-toothed squirrel from the *Ice Age* movie and I slowly made it to the end of the journey. Nina was sleeping during the night and she only woke up once around three a.m. and felt the need to move around in the car.

My dream was becoming real, until around midday, when something happened. The apartment we booked via Airbnb looked promising, we unpacked our stuff and took a nap. Already then I began to feel unwell. Then we went for a little stroll around the area and my sickness got worse. My bowels started to burn and I ended up running to the toilet for the first time.

All right, perhaps my body just needs to acclimatise. I go once and then it will be fine, I thought to myself. Unfortunately for me, that didn't happen. Afternoon swimming and an evening stroll ended once again with a bathroom visit, from where I didn't move until late. There was no reason for me to leave the bathroom, since the intervals between my runs to the bathroom were approximately three minutes long. The situation got so much worse, that I decided to take a pill in order to get some sleep and continue with my bowel clearance in the morning.

The combination of 'bowel blocking', clay and litres of liquid, diet and a good sleep worked well. Next day the frequency of my bowel movement rapidly decreased and in the afternoon the shit was gone.

Nevertheless, I spent a day in bed. I was weak, hungry and rather tired, although I felt admittedly detoxified. I still kept the same diet the following day, I made myself a chicken broth and observed tourists stuffing themselves with local cuisine. Next day my holiday could finally commence. I swam in the beautiful sea, we took a walk in the evening followed up with a light meal that finally tasted like food flavours.

I started to enjoy the holiday and recalled my dream from my early days of parenthood. Until the third day, when my wife and her mother started to have enough of each other. There was a deluge of negative emotions in the air and the apartment sometimes felt like a mental ward. Luckily for me, I have the ability to penetrate emotions in grown-ups, which allowed me to continue living my dream and not pay too much attention the arguing.

Nina's turn came when she decided her new tooth was going to start coming in and with it came her old grumpy mood, and then it happened. While I was changing her nappies, Nina accidentally scratched my eye with her long nails, which haven't been cut for a week.

Anything I have ever experienced before was nowhere near as painful as this. It's that sort of feeling when someone scratches your eye out, but the nerves still function well and keep your mind informed on how painful this is. And then someone starts to cut your eye with a razor, or imagine you have a piece of steel in your eye and you can't get it out. And when the wind blows and the sun starts to shine, everything gets a thousand times worse.

When being by the sea, it's quite a usual thing for the sun to shine and for the wind to blow. I was brave enough to go out for dinner suffering from horrendous pain only to end up at an emergency room with an eye plaster, a bill for having my eye rinsed with salt water, a written referral to see an eye specialist and a prescription for antibiotics.

Needless to say, the night was horrific and I had no idea what the following day would look like or how bad the pain was going to be. I was thinking about how we were going to get home, whether I will be able to see properly, how long will the injury take to heal and whether I will have to undergo surgery.

It has never happened to me before, so please don't laugh. The doctor told me to have a check-up, I sincerely hope she was talking about my eye. Luckily enough, my cornea performed some heroic actions and the next day all the pain went away. Even though my vision was blurred, I didn't feel any pain. I spent another day in the apartment resting and sleeping, because my healthy eye felt pretty worn out since it had to do all the work by itself. In the evening I took the bandage off and started to be somewhat productive again.

During the last third of our perfect family holiday my vision was still blurred, but I was able to see. I went to the beach, had a swim and enjoyed some delicious meals. Me and my wife had a moment alone in the evening and we went for a nice dinner and a stroll on the beach, while my mother-in-law was looking after Nina. I felt very grateful for this. We soon started to get ready for the night journey back and this time we were on our way around four p.m. We kept stopping every hour and a half because Nina wanted to stretch around the car and eat, until we could be on our way again.

Compared to our departure, the return journey was significantly more dramatic, including Nina's twenty-minute-long hysterical breakdown. **Final conclusion: the holiday was very different from how I had originally pictured it in my dream. I was pleased to be back home and I was looking forward to getting back to our established system that we all got used to. Despite all the inconveniences, I felt relaxed, stronger and determined with no concerns about usual stuff, since I had to prioritize my own physical well-being. It made me think, read and think again and be able to perform in a better mood.**

For nearly a week after coming back from our holiday I was testing new dietary habits as well as a slightly modified working schedule and my conceptual framework. I do everything with much joy, despite the fact that our key work project requires significant effort and great patience. On the other hand, it's business and nothing comes from nothing. If you assume you are all set and from now on the business will blossom, prepare yourself that there will always be some kind of an issue or a risk you may have to deal with it.

As for Nina, there is a lot of fun involved, as well as our ever-growing responsibility. She appears to be a rather smart and clever baby and she is currently determined to examine the use of her own voice when negotiating. She objects loudly when not getting her way (mostly we don't even have a clue what this could be). When she is taken out of the bath a moment earlier than she actually wants, she starts crying hysterically. Every time there is something she dislikes, her attitude gets immediately shared with us. And believe me, it's not an easy thing to refuse anything to such a small creature.

She is fully aware of what the word ENOUGH means and she understands the serious facial expressions of her parents rather well. Despite all this, she can smile so beautifully, she gives kisses and has learned to crawl pretty well by now. She can get up on her legs, lean on her knees, sit up and she talks all the time. She can say words, understands very well what is going on and she can serve herself some food.

Chapter 17
TWELFTH MONTH: A YEAR I SHALL NEVER FORGET

With this month, I decided to end my book and whatever comes next is a part of a different story and a different book. By now, I have pretty well transformed myself into the role of a father, who has left the thought of having only one child behind and decided he could handle another baby.

Life would be boring without new challenges, and this could be a new challenge on my journey through life. The second baby could come perhaps in about three years, so that Nina could first comfortably start the next new chapter in her life when she attends a nursery school.

Life goes fast and our Nina crawls around like a little dragon and soon she won't be able to keep up with the inevitable speed just with her knees and hands. She leans towards furniture, falls on her butt and sometimes even on her head. The sound of her head hitting the floor every time she falls over seems like a rumble in the factory.

From time to time, she storms into the room yelling, although she is very well aware of what's appropriate and what isn't. She constantly examines, tries out and discovers new things. She grows smarter with every new day and every day brings us something new. But what's more, she is a great partner in crime.

Finally, the time has come for me to be able to return to my childhood and cause a lot of mischief with my daughter, which she loves very much. Everything still requires an immense amount of effort with very little time for ourselves. Besides, I have to take over from her mother from time to time to let her have some fun, otherwise she might go insane from all that constant being on alert, changing nappies, soothing and lisping. Our once reckless life only filled with work and rest is inevitably over.

The days will come when our children will become overwhelmed by their own life that overtakes the boring and uninteresting life of grown-ups.

According to more experienced parents this will happen sooner than you think, although for the next five years it will be some sort of a craziness. Already, even now, at the turn of Nina's first year, we still undergo many dramatic improvements and breakthroughs. To name some examples, for the past three months our daughter goes to sleep at one p.m. and five p.m. and she tends to sleep for an hour to an hour and a half.

But then something happens and she starts to complain loudly. I soothe her and wait until she falls asleep. All I wish for is to get some rest, but staying by her side only makes things harder. Everything that caused her pain and crying (caused mostly by her growing teeth) is over, but to my dismay the baby still refuses to cope with the fact that she can get back to normal.

She would rather prefer the way it was before, when her poor mother was getting cramps all over her body, caused by the discomfort of leaning over the bed until Nina falls asleep. Eventually it always ended up with tears anyway. It must be rather hard for anyone to be able to stand without any discomfort, no matter their age or how many yoga lessons they attend every week.

During the second vaccination, Nina's reaction was much worse. Her skin reacted with a red swelling bump, which completely ruined her otherwise great mood for another couple of days. She was all tears, weeping and generally annoyed by all the chemicals in her blood. Regardless of everybody's discomfort and due to the general moral well-being of this planet, this vaccination had to be done.

BACK TO THE FOREST

The night before our daughter's celebration of her first year on earth, we left on our second holiday. We drove to a mountain cottage with very basic facilities, set deep in the forest. A very different environment compared to the one especially built for tourists, where we went earlier this summer.

Such a family holiday felt very rewarding and so relaxing, even though after having shared one bed (one hundred and fifty by two hundred centimetres) with my two girls, around three a.m. I decided to relocate myself to the sofa in the living room, in order to get some rest. Our journey to the relatively backward and poor region reminded me about some real-life priorities.

Social interaction with others and a need to conform to certain rules within a community instead of aiming to follow our own individual path, has a beneficial impact on both grown-ups and children. Even though our daughter is not able to fully appreciate it yet, we will do our best in the future to include more such experiences in her life. This relaxing environment and breathtakingly pristine nature makes you change your entire mindset.

Suddenly it doesn't matter who likes what and who hates something else, who shared a post online, what is falling apart where and which companies have filed for bankruptcy. You breathe the fresh air, drink clean water, have somewhere to live and you are surrounded by your loved ones. You have all the happiness in the world.

Being a great fan of technology, creating digital products and IT systems, this family holiday away from the Internet grid is exactly what I needed in terms of seeking perfect harmony without having to constantly socialise with the modern society. All of this will have a positive impact on good mental health and a great education of our daughter.

To celebrate Nina's first birthday, we organised a small party. Ever since she was born, the entire world has changed for us and became more beautiful. At first, I lost myself somewhere at the very beginning of my journey as a parent, I was holding hands with a tiny shouting creature which soon turned my life upside down. There was no way of preparing myself for such experience, as much as I tried to be a loving and caring father as soon as she arrived, I was unable to fully achieve it.

Mother Nature gave women hormones to help them overcome the worst and unfold their motherly love. Whereas men, not being as fortunate as women, received something that appears to be an old laboratory, ready to explode any time. This is why men seek different ways to deal with such unexpectedly new and different situation, for they can only operate through their own intellectual thinking. Just like with any sport, business or in your entire life, you have to hang on and fight, and work on yourself as a father, husband, and the person who keeps the family financially stable.

Arnold Schwarzenegger's motto, "No pain, no gain" is a life philosophy, there is no success without a failure. These words make me finalise this book with a suitable title: **Opportunities.**

MAKE THE WORLD A BETTER PLACE

It happens time and time again, as centuries pass, on every continent and to all human races. The higher the country's civilisation status, the bigger the problems. People are inclined to give up easily, with a lack of sense of responsibility or commitments, and whenever problems call for a solution, they run away elsewhere, chasing something or someone. With every birth comes a very dramatic change in one's entire lifestyle and their priorities.

Everything that was previously of any importance to you has completely lost its sense and what used to be taken for granted is no longer available. Your inner self is about to change into something resembling a large cooking pot while you have to keep the water replenishing to prevent the pot from exploding. Both you and your partner decide on how well you cope with these dramatic changes and how you learn to work with them. After having observed the world and my environment, I found out there are two following paths. This transition into a family life will either make your relationship stronger and bolder, or it will lead you to a break up. Throughout this book I intended to precisely describe all my feelings and the mental states I have experienced on my journey to being a parent with a successful job background. I wouldn't say I was either too fast or too slow in this process, it took me just as long as it should.

Throughout my years in high school, I worked very hard, with as little as four hours of sleep a night and as the end of my studies approached, I managed to sell my company which lead me to a big financial growth at an early stage of my life. Such reality, in fact, might have had some negative effect on my personality as well, since I became acquainted to somewhat higher standards and began to take many things which have little to no importance in life for granted. With this in mind, when Nina came to this world and her physiological needs became my priority, the upper two-thirds of Maslow's hierarchy of needs have completely changed and the conflict of interest began to occur. A conflict of interest is very common in the modern world, you don't have to think about being hungry or finding a place to stay, worry about warmth or keeping yourself safe. The basics of the hierarchy have a solid base.

In the third segment of the hierarchy is where we start to struggle. Today, we lavishly spend our time on Facebook, Snapchat or Instagram and most of the time we don't even know our social media friends personally. We break up via WhatsApp and have absolutely no ability to withstand problems within the community. We lack problem-solving skills and many times we even refuse to acknowledge personal criticism.

We live with our parents stuck behind computers until we turn thirty while spending money on useless things with little to no interest in becoming a good parent in future. Despite all this, only one hundred and fifty years ago as many as ten people were living under one roof in a small cottage. They knew nothing but their own small community and hard work and had nothing to care for except their loved ones.

Remind yourself about this when you're feeling down and when it may seem you are standing outside the gates of hell and that all you had inevitably disappeared, because it's not like this at all. **One has to make a few steps back to be able to appreciate what is yet awaiting.** Fighting towards having a great family and a strong relationship is the highest value of all. All possessions and statuses will be gone, but your memories and your love will stay. **Albert Einstein said, "The reason we are here is for others, especially the ones whose smile and welfare our own life depends on."**

Enjoy it. Yours faithfully, David Vais.

Chapter 18
EPILOGUE

My time plan was clear: twelve months. I must admit I had a rather precise idea about how the book would be written ever since I first began to think about it. My aim was not to scribble down every single utterance from Nina, word by word, or record every time she passed gas or fell over. At the same time, neither did I wish to spend ten years collecting odds and ends, only to come up with a sort of helter-skelter stream-of-consciousness story. My real goal was to develop myself into a great modern dad and achieve that within twelve months, as well as to describe my new daddy adventures to others. In my opinion, I have successfully reached my goal.

Twelve months have elapsed since I finished the book in Czech. Once again, that magical number twelve. And since we are just now adding the finishing touches to the paperback release, I set aside some time to provide you with a few additional father-daughter moments from the past year: Nina's second twelve months. Undoubtedly, you may be wondering whether I've changed my point of view in any way. To be bluntly honest, the answer is yes, I have. The first year of constant discovery and infantile battles provided a foundation for the following year. Perhaps I should start with a story about our second 'perfect' summer holiday.

As I lie here in a cosy Croatian bed, little Nina is enjoying her afternoon nap and my wife has taken over the couch to watch YouTube videos. This time, though, my eyesight is perfect and, so far, I haven't had to turn the bathroom into my bedroom, either (well, apart from that time I had to suddenly dash off to the toilet as a result of drinking an unpasteurised Croatian dairy product). All in all, we've been having a splendid time, despite a truly hideous vacation start. As we were preparing ourselves for the rather long road journey to our holiday resort, Nina had trouble falling asleep and woke up extremely unhappy for no earthy reason only an hour later.

It was Nina's way of loudly expressing her displeasure (often exceeding a hundred decibels), that encouraged me to leap out of bed just when I had hoped to get some sleep before beginning our drive to the Adriatic coast. Oh, how I despise driving all night over long distances! (Of course, we had a good reason not to travel by air, which would have been much more comfortable, but that's a long story.) And since I was already awake, it seemed like a good idea to discuss our next move. Considering all the possible reasons for Nina's obvious discontent, my wife and I concluded that whatever the reason for her emotional despair – possibly even the flu coming on – we decided to set off on our vacation trip.

Shortly after we were on the road, Nina began to demonstrate her extreme displeasure with our decision and continued to shriek and cry so hysterically that I quite frankly almost made a U-turn and would have cancelled the entire holiday. Unfortunately for us, I didn't and the entire car trip continued exactly as it began. Nina had simply decided it was a better idea to stay awake and complain loudly rather than to take a calm nap in her car seat. Over the next several hours, her hysterics slowly reached deafening levels.

The situation grew even worse approximately seventy-five kilometres before reaching our destination, when all she would say was, "No, no, no, down, down, down!" If I may translate, this basically means, "Get me out of this horrible car seat, I won't stay here any longer. I want to sit on the back seat or on Mommy's lap." Even though my wife tried her best to convince Nina that we would be arriving shortly and explained how dangerous it would be to let her crawl around the car at a hundred and thirty kilometres, it was all to no avail.

Approximately twenty-eight kilometers from our final destination, Nina's crying was so intense that not even all of Kim Jong-un's weapons of mass destruction could have been louder than she was. Finally, upon our arrival at the desired destination, I was so exhausted, I was hardly able to concentrate on our conversation with the apartment owner. It had taken over an hour to calm Nina down and finally fall asleep in her car seat.

So it might seem that from now on going forward everything was just perfect and we enjoyed our long-awaited vacation, right? Actually, not really. That first night Nina began to suffer from a dry cough. She was wheezing until three a.m., which meant that she couldn't sleep and a genuine case of the flu started coming on, as well. It was that evil watery-type flu, the one that keeps you awake at night due to breathing difficulties and excessive mucus, which tends to spread all over your face like the Nile Delta. So, once again, we began considering the alternatives. Should we turn around and go home or try to handle it in Croatia? Since we had prepared for the possibility of all types of infections, we had packed a wide variety of medications to take with us, including a nasal aspirator (also known as a baby snot sucker) for mucus, we eventually decided to stay despite Nina's symptoms. The next two nights were disastrous in terms of trying to get any sleep, but everything was quite fine during the day. Nina hardly coughed at all and we were having a lovely time with friends who were staying nearby. But that all changed rapidly at night.

As if Nina's illness wasn't bad enough, I started to feel unwell, too, and wasn't able to breathe through my nose at night. Three days into our holiday, the weather conditions also changed dramatically. Instead of swimming in the sea, a weather front sent us large amounts of rain pouring down from heavy dark clouds, flooding the streets and dropping egg-sized hailstones to smash the car. After two days of torrential downpours, the promised warm and sunny Croatian summer turned into cold, empty beaches and chilly, gloomy days that never got above twenty degrees.

If I were someone who loves to spend my time at the seaside, I would have most likely ended up on antidepressants, cursing the whole world and in particular mediocre Croatian tourist services that were, of course, available for 'very reasonable' prices. But, you know what? I didn't mind one bit. The reason we chose Croatia as our destination was our fondness of their relatively clean ocean, which is beneficial to our bodies. Our primary aim was not to waste our time sunbathing among hundreds of rather plump tourists (after all, who the hell has time to go to the fitness studio when they're working?).

The main reason we went to Croatia was to swim in the clear sea waters and enjoy somewhat good food, but mostly to get away from constantly ringing telephones, a deluge of emails and continuous online chats. Happily, the trip did have that satisfying result. The fact that none of us felt entirely well and everyone suffered from coughing and sneezing didn't have any serious negative effects on our overall enjoyment of the vacation break. Generally speaking, we got what we needed in terms of contentment and a sense of general well-being. In terms of a perfect dream holiday, it's something very individual and really depends on whatever your priorities are.

The entire previous year had been a great example of this: Nina's second year on earth. By the time I'd finished writing the last words concerning her twelfth month, we discovered we had a toddler. She was a rather smart toddler, I must admit, although still a toddler. When your child begins to sway and stumble through the toddler stage, there aren't many particularly major physiological developments to go with it. While an infant is still tiny, it can't really do much until it can finally stand up on its own. Then everything speeds up. At about one year of age, your toddler is able to pull itself up, sway about a bit and fall down, but soon learns to walk and even run around more-or-less steadily and with a little help can even climb up and down the stairs while holding onto something – or someone.

Our Nina started to walk pretty well at about fourteen months. She was soon able to run and jump even better than arthritic elderly people in TV commercials can. Still, a child's physical development is fairly unremarkable during its second year, except of course the significant milestone of the last and long-awaited baby tooth. That final bloody tooth!

For the most part, we managed to get through Nina's initial teething period with relative ease. Luckily for us, by the end of the first year, we'd already been through all the minor trouble that goes along with it. Sometimes she'd have a slight temperature or cry about the gum pain, but there was nothing major. However, when Nina's back teeth began to come in, the situation was quite the opposite. We had it all: high fever, nausea and hysterical crying throughout several nights. But, thank heavens, all her teeth have come out now. Next, however, we noticed some abrupt breakthroughs in Nina's intellectual development.

Actually, it was more her character that went through some important developmental changes. Nina experienced her second Christmas at the age of fourteen months, carefully observing all the Christmas lights and gazing with astonishment at the lavishly decorated Christmas tree. She didn't seem to pay a lot of attention to unwrapping any presents and, in fact, only took a slight interest in that activity for a very short time, much like an elderly man may occasionally concern himself with his prostate (this may be an inappropriate comparison, but it's where we'll all end up at some point in our lives). From a parental point of view, we still hadn't reached the desired high point in our baby's life. Nina's second birthday party, however, was completely different.

Then she was screaming for joy, literally tearing the wrapping paper off her biggest birthday present and partying with her three-year-old cousin to the sound of the biggest hits of contemporary pop music. Her endless enthusiasm and the ability to share her excitement and moments of pure happiness with the world. Her thrills, love and the pure and powerful energy that floats around her, help to keep us motivated during the darker and less enjoyable stages of her character development.

According to most of the books you read, your child's growing truculence is part of a toddler's first realisation of its ability to express refusal. In other words, these experts explain this phase as the first expression of independent juvenile behaviour and claim it lasts until your child is about three years of age. Don't believe it! It is merely wishful thinking. Nina learned the secret magic of the word, 'No!' very well during her first twenty months on earth. Ever since then, she has made it quite perfectly clear that she is fully aware of her new skill and is prepared to use it accordingly. Aside from her newly acquired skill, she also came up with a great forceful artistry – the art of the tantrum – which she finds comes in rather handy to her. I call her tantrums, 'Phelps'. She rolls onto her stomach, kicking and punching whatever is in reach of her fists to underscore her demands.

And don't ever dare attempt to ask this baby girl for a kiss. You'll still get one, but usually spontaneously in a sudden outburst of love, and often unexpectedly during one of her favourite activities. However, as she becomes more clever, you'll get your kiss at those times when your baby is trying to try to achieve some personal goal. For example, our Nina is perfectly aware of what she's after – most of the time pretty much anything and everything. It may be an ice cream, preferably immediately, to be followed by another one a moment later, and a third one to follow. A new bear, a new ball or a little boat might be alternatives. Or Dad's phone, some random guy's phone or the tablet of a little girl whose acquaintance she just made in a coffee shop.

At this point, 'No', is simply not an answer, any more. Instead it's become a starting point for aggressive negotiations that usually result in a loud protest of opposition and the so-called, 'Phelps' or 'panda' posture, when Nina sits on the floor, twists her feet and suddenly rips off her shoes and throws them in a corner. My wife and I have therefore come to the following conclusion: under no circumstances are we to use the word 'No' when it comes to Nina's upbringing. Even though this sometimes drives both of us insane, we try our very best to understand Nina's displeasure and talk her out of it.

"Nina, wave goodbye to the bear. There are plenty of toys at home waiting for you, including your favourite mouse. We will come back to say hello to the bear another time."

"Nina, we will buy another ice cream tomorrow. Two ice creams are enough for today because you could get a stomach ache." It would be more than a slight exaggeration to claim that this works perfectly every time, as there are days she refuses to do without her 'Phelps' or 'panda'. Despite the many evil looks we tend to get when Nina publicly proceeds with her 'Phelps', we try not to let her have her way. For a little while we let her go on with her hysterics, and then slowly but surely start taking over the initiative and offer a compromise. Certainly, there are often times when no explanations or discussions with an angry two-year-old prove to be useful, and that is when we take the approach of a slightly more strict attitude.

To a certain extent, there are plenty of suggestions and opinions on how to bring up a child to be found in various books and magazines. I've read a great many of them myself. Thousands of pages filled with information on how to precisely explain or demonstrate your initiative are the main topic of them all, which I agree with. Without a doubt, inane commands and orders, constantly snapping at your child and being patronising (you're just a kid, I'm your parent and you will obey and behave), isn't exactly the most convenient way to raise your child.

With every new day, my wife and I understand more deeply how rewarding this way of upbringing actually is, a form of child raising that a Czech author named Marek Herman hugely supports. It draws on a deep compassion and higher comprehension of a child's various means of expressing its feelings, which are closely related to character development. On the other hand, being defenders of many of the good 'old school' methods, my wife and I have the aim of setting clear boundaries and sticking with them. Not only does our Nina need lots of room to discover her inner self, she also needs to understand how far to push the boundaries... and where to stop trying to get her own way by force.

All in all, life with a tiny two-year-old creature is admittedly both physically and mentally exhausting and requires much more effort than the life we had shared with a one-year-old baby. Sometimes both my wife and I inconceivably shrug our shoulders when we recall how we were convinced that it was almost impossible to teach our little five-month-old baby girl any discipline. Back then, Nina was unable to run away from us and there was no danger of needing to buy out an entire grocery store. However, at the same time, this new life with such a wonderful little creature is so fulfilling and exciting that I wouldn't change a thing.

I love my family from the bottom of my heart. I deeply love my daughter and I'm in love with my wife. My greatest difficulty sometimes is to provide both of them with enough love and enough empathy, especially because making a partnership work requires the ability to support and show compassion towards each other throughout even the most difficult times. In particular, there is the need to share moments alone with your wife as well as to recharge your batteries on a family holiday. Nevertheless, the moments when I used to recall how our old life consisted of only the two of us, when our sleep was never interrupted and we made spontaneous decisions, are long past. I cannot even remember what that memory felt like, and – to be honest – I don't feel the need of remembering that feeling any more. My life has changed. It's been given a brand new meaning and entered another, completely new and different dimension. I'm happy right here, right now. It is no longer my aim to just experience life through the birth of my second baby, it is to truly enjoy it to the fullest. It will certainly be difficult at times, we know that already, but despite that, my wife and I really hope to have another child. And perhaps another after that. My family has become the epicentre of my whole life and world.

I hope from the bottom of my heart you find the same sense of satisfaction as a father. I hope that you can accept every day's setbacks as your personal challenge and that they will help you in making the world around you a better place. There is no doubt in my mind that we are quite likely living in the most advanced age in human history. Pessimists probably only see the financial precipice ahead of us, international refugee crises, Trump, Brexit, an insane North Korean dictator, widespread droughts, floods and polluted oceans.

Except that there is no longer a Hitler rampaging across Europe, nor are millions of people dying from diseases like cholera or the Black Death. Affordable health care is widely available in much of the world and through the power of social media, people are aware of the needs of the underprivileged in developing countries everywhere, which is leading to support for a broad range of humanitarian organisations and private charities. Ideally, we could all have access to endless supplies of drinking water, as well as electrical power. Although some aspects of modern life have detrimental effects on our earth, there is still so much more to be discovered and carried out to make life better for people all over the world.

Oftentimes we worry unnecessarily and make arrangements for problems that will never occur. Maybe we would be better off reducing the number of rules and regulations we place on ourselves. But actually, we should realise that we are really rather fortunate. Living in Europe enables us to do and say anything we like. It is up to us what we are going to do with our freedom and how we decide to pursue our life's goals. We have almost a boundless selection of choices open to us. So many possibilities, in fact, that we often have difficulty making up our minds which to choose.

What a strange paradox that in such situations we tend to recall the old adage that, 'The family is the basic unit of society', as well as the foundation for building our future. How tolerant future generations will be, how well our descendants will achieve solidarity with one another, to what extent succeeding generations will protect and sustain our wonderful planet earth by establishing responsible policies and obeying reasonable rules – that will depend both on us and on how well we raise our children. That is possibly the most frightening thing about becoming a first-time parent: we are the role models for our children.

The decisions we make and the actions we take will blaze a trail and set us all on a huge variety of possible paths that will lead to the highest levels of development achievable by human beings. But, by the same token, poor choices we make could also result in sowing the seeds of unimaginable ecological and natural disasters. When we accept the responsibility for bringing children into this unpredictable world, we are demonstrating our courage and confidence that we can help create a more just and fair society for children born everywhere on our amazing planet. We are showing through our commitment to our families that we believe a better world is possible in the long-term. Of course, to reach that goal, we must teach our children to prudently only exploit our habitat in moderation and to always consider the environmental impact of their decisions on the lives of their own children and their progeny.

If we teach our children to share – meaning the planet's wealth and their possessions – as well as knowledge, emotions and commitment to the well-being of others, we can hope that there will not only be less waste and pollution, but also that the world will become less stressful. However, to reach that point, we must first – and most importantly – learn and accept that being a parent is an enormous gift. Having children should never be seen as an unwanted burden or in some way a hindrance to finding personal happiness and fulfilment. At the end of the day, it is our children who give our life a purpose and make it truly fulfilling. When we became dads, we were given our chance. So, let's enjoy it to the fullest!